JUV     Unkelbach, Kurt.
SF
426.5    The best-of-breeds
.U53      guide for young dog
Cop. 1    lovers

7.95

| DATE | | | |
|---|---|---|---|
| | | | |
| | | | |
| | | | |
| | | | |
| | | | |
| | | | |
| | | | |
| | | | |
| | | | |
| | | | |
| | | | |
| | | | |
| | | | |

# ABOUT THE BOOK

Candid, factual and entertaining, this book is indispensable for dog lovers who are about to become owners for the first time, or for second- or third-time owners who have been disappointed with the dogs they've owned in the past. Whatever your status, the pages reveal whether you should *really* own a dog, and the average costs you can anticipate in terms of food, health, care, and equipment.

Then, on to the best bets in dogs. Of the 200 or so pure breeds trotting around in the United States and Canada, the author has selected thirty-eight with the young dog-owner specifically in mind. These choices—plus the Americanis, a new name for an old, unfinished breed—come in a wide range of sizes, coats, colors, talents and appetites.

Among the pre-ownership subjects explored and explained are important tips on locating the right breeder, what to look for in the dog before you buy, and how to find a quality pup at no cost. Then, there is foolproof advice on the care, proper feeding, and easy housebreaking and training of your dog.

For those who aspire to be more than just a dog owner, the pages remove the mystique of dog shows and Obedience trials in addition to providing inside information on the likeliest careers in the dog world. And so much more. All you really need to know about selecting, understanding, training and loving your dog.

# BEST-OF-BREEDS GUIDE FOR YOUNG DOG LOVERS

## BY KURT UNKELBACH

G. P. Putnam's Sons, New York

## BOOKS BY KURT UNKELBACH

The American Dog Book
Uncle Charlie's Poodle
Love on a Leash
Those Lovable Retrievers
The Pleasures of Dog Ownership (with Evie Unkelbach)
Albert Payson Terhune: The Master of Sunnybank
The Winning of Westminster
The Dog in My Life
Murphy
How to Bring Up Your Pet Dog
How to Show Your Dog and Win
How to Make Money in Dogs
The Dog Who Never Knew
Ruffian: International Champion
Both Ends of the Leash: Selecting & Training Your Dog
You're a Good Dog, Joe: Knowing & Training Your Puppy
Catnip: Selecting & Training Your Cat
Tiger Up a Tree: Knowing & Training Your Kitten
A Cat and His Dogs

Clumber Spaniel pup at eight weeks, courtesy of the breeders, Mr. and Mrs. William Lloyd, Beau Chien Kennels, Canada.

LIBRARY OF CONGRESS CATALOGING IN PUBLICATION DATA
Unkelbach, Kurt.
The best-of-breeds guide for young dog lovers.
Includes index. SUMMARY: Describes thirty-eight pure breeds,
discusses canine training, care, breeding, and equipment,
and provides information on the world of the dog fancier.
1. Dogs—Juvenile literature. 2. Dog breeds—Juvenile literature.
[1. Dogs. 2. Dog breeds] I. Title.
SF426.5.U53    636.7'1    77-13346
ISBN 0-399-20622-1

# Contents

# Appreciations

I am indebted to those owners, breeders, exhibitors, handlers, judges, breed club secretaries and canine historians whose facts, insights and photographs are found on the pages of this book. It is possible to say that the validity of this work is based on personal experiences—although many of those experiences were not mine.

Finding the right photographs of good dogs to illustrate the breeds was much more difficult than anticipated. While top-flight purebreds are not rare, proper photographs of them are—if you agree with me that a dog should be able to hold up head and tail without human assistance.

The long and often frustrating hunt for suitable photographs was conducted by my wife, Evie, who found what we wanted at leading kennels in the United States and Canada. My special thanks to her and the individuals named in the captions.

K.U.

# 1

# So You Want to Own a Dog?

At one time or another just about everybody wants to own a dog. This is a fact of life in many countries, but in America it is almost a way of life—so much so that people who are brave enough to admit no interest in ownership find themselves regarded by dog lovers as unpatriotic nitwits who should be denied credit cards and seats on the bus.

Still, it's high time somebody said a few words in defense of those castigated, for some are teachers and dentists and dance teachers who are just as sensible and socially acceptable as their critics, who are also often teachers and dentists and dance teachers and always dog lovers. Those about to be defended realize this sad truth: some people should not own dogs. To put it bluntly, they lack the qualities required for a reasonably good human-animal relationship.

Now let's look at some of the critics and consider this sadder truth: some people who shouldn't own dogs, do. Deep in their hearts, all are first-rate dog lovers, but they possess one or more disqualifying personality traits that would be deemed unacceptable by any sensible canine.

A dog just doesn't stand a chance of achieving his true pet potential if his owner—or the person he spends most of his time with (and thus amounts to his owner in his eyes)—is a nervous wreck, short-tempered, cruel, or impatient and overly demanding. Perfectionists are always poor bets as owners; so are the irresponsibles; and let's not forget those otherwise charming owners who keep overestimating the intelligence and capabilities of their charges. Behind closed doors, they have been known to relieve their disappointments with kicks directed at their bewildered canine friends.

Roll them all together—the good dog-lovers and the bad—and they own an estimated total of 41 million* pet dogs, give or take a few hundred thousand. Whatever the real figure, this estimate makes the United States the doggiest country in the world and it's the figure used by advertisers of products for canines (foods, flea powders, toys, etc.) at budget time.

While the researchers do agree on the approximate total of 41 million dogs, they have been unable to settle on the number of families owning dogs. However, nine out of ten dog-food-company executives believe that at least one out of every three families owns one or more dogs, and all are doing their best to push the statistic to better than two out of three families.

Well, to keep those twenty-three-million-plus families happy, and to insure a ready supply of pooches for newcomers, the puppy whelping rate has been running along at about two thousand pups per hour, day and night, every day. These days, a slim majority of the pups are purebreds, and while almost all of the breeding that produces them is planned, not all of the tail-wagging results are worth celebrating. Just under half of the new pups are nonpurebreds and are generally regarded as mongrels, although technically some are crossbreeds (see Glossary). The breeding behind mongrels is usually unplanned and accidental, in the sense that the dogs who mated did not seek the permission of their owners or even wait for a formal introduction.

---

*This estimate does not include homeless dogs such as strays, or feral, or unowned dogs in residence at humane shelters. Add those and the total canine population of the United States is close to 60 million.

As with purebreds, some mongrels make extremely good pets and some don't, and frequently the owners make the difference, although they may not even know it. The only real disadvantage to owning a mongrel is that the dog will never be eligible to compete in the sports of the American Kennel Club, which is dedicated to the advancement of purebred dogs and not likely to change. This permanent ineligibility does not alter the mongrel's credentials as a true *Canis familiaris*, the social animal who is just as gung ho as humans for family life, and is often superior in many ways to the nearest Poodle.

We are not gathered on these pages to dictate your choice of purebred or mongrel, but to offer guidelines about the best pure breeds for first-time owners—or second- and third-time owners who have been disappointed with the dogs they've owned so far. If your breed choice is right, and you are willing and able to accept certain long-run responsibilities, your dog will become one of the best friends you'll ever have. But if you don't give your dog a break, he'll probably turn into more of a nuisance than a friend—a pest rather than a pet.

You give your dog a break by always extending yourself, always going more than halfway. Forget the pedigree and the promises of the breeder. A dog is not as capable as he looks, or as bright as he may seem, and he is always much more dependent on his owner than he'd care to admit. For a rewarding relationship with your pooch, it's best to forget the fifty-fifty theme music that's usually in the background of a successful relationship between people (friendship, business, marriage) and realize that you must always be top banana with your dog. You must care for him, and educate and train him, but he won't be able to reciprocate in kind.

If you possess the willingness to go more than halfway, you are probably a walking example of the virtues that take the risk out of dog ownership. Risk for the dog, that is. You are patient, understanding and forgiving, and you do not believe in miracles or in cruelties to animals. While you don't need all of those qualities to be a dog lover, they'll come in handy—and be appreciated by the canine of your choice—when you decide to take the logical step and become a dog owner. And if you're allergic to dog hairs, don't despair. Your doctor can probably help you, and if that's news to the doctor, a nearby veterinarian should be able to recommend a medic who has the answers.

If what you *are* is important, where you live is only a major concern if you're a city dweller. While the canine does adjust to almost any environment inhabited by people, the Lord didn't have the city in mind when he invented the beast, and humans still haven't developed an ideal municipal breed. By accident rather than design, a few breeds are top choices for city life (at least from an owner's viewpoint), and they are among the candidates to be surveyed on these pages. With the exception of the pint-sized canines who stay in the pink of condition by dashing around a room, jumping from chair to table to shelf and then diving into a tank of tropical fish, a dog has a very hard time getting sufficient exercise in the city. A canine will not get enough strolling on a leash—even if the stroll lasts all day.

Time is also a consideration—your time. While there's a right pup for you and finding him (or her) shouldn't be much of a task, he's not going to satisfy you if you give him short shrift. The more he's in your company, the greater his devotion to you and the keener his desire to please. All during his important growing period (the first ten months) the pup's personality is being shaped. You can mold that personality pretty much as you please, but not by mere wishful thinking and never *in absentia*.

Since every pup requires her own amount of human companionship and tutoring, and owner A has more free time than owner B and less than owner C. not even a firm ruling by the Supreme Court on *Required Time to Spend With Pup* would be much help. But in the spirit of giving your dog a break and going more than halfway, it's only proper to share more than fifty percent of your free time with her and not fair to count sleeping time—when you are under the blanket and she's on top of it—as free time.

Obviously, the pup can't be with you during school hours, but she can be quiet company during all those study hours you spend at home. If you hold down a job, she can't be with you, but she can certainly trot at your heels and keep out of the way sometimes as you attend to assigned chores at home. And if you're a social butterfly, you'll just have to fit the pup into some of your engagements or cancel them.

Whether the pup in your life arrives as a gift or as a purchase, ownership of a dog will require continued fiscal responsibility on somebody's part, and the pooch won't care if that somebody is you, your parents, or sweet Aunt Tillie. Here's how most of the money goes:

**Food.** It is more economical to buy prepared dog food than it is to purchase the necessary ingredients and then mix and stew them. Commercial foods come as dry (bagged), semimoist (packaged), and wet (canned). While prices vary depending on brands and where you live, the best economy diet consists mostly of dry with a touch of wet. Where I live in New England (near a city of thirty thousand and with a twenty-minute drive to my feed store), I could feed a fifty-pound adult dog on quality-brand foods for about $3 per week. I can and do feed my sixty- to seventy-pounders on less, because I practice certain thrifty tricks.

More about food costs, what to look for in nutrition, how to read a label, and other related information on the pages up ahead. Here and now it is only necessary to know that two dogs of the same breed and of identical weights will not necessarily require the same amount of food to stay healthy. Still, the average fifty-pounder can be fed on $3 per week, and cut that in half for the average twenty-five-pounder.

Keep in mind that those figures are for adult dogs of one year and older who have achieved, or just about achieved, maximum size. With the exception of the toy breeds (who mature earlier, often at six months), it costs more to feed any dog during the first twelve months. All during this growing span, a pup needs more food and has no trouble stashing it away. If $3.00 per week is the adult estimate, figure on $4.50 per week for the first nine months, then pennies less each week over the next three months.

**Veterinarian.** Next to you, the nearest friendly veterinarian will be your dog's second most important person. While vet fees are as variable as the weather, it is safe to predict that they are higher in the city than in the country, the reason being overhead, not talent. The dollars noted here are the ones I pay to my vet for services rendered, and they might not hold true in your locality. Here are my basic vet costs for a pup:

1. Temporary shot. If the dam is healthy, her pup inherits about six weeks of immunity from canine diseases. After that, he needs a shot. Usually, and depending on the breeder's intelligence, a pup gets this shot ($9) several weeks before he's sold. It continues his immunity until he gets the following:

2. Permanent shots. Two shots, usually given four weeks apart, the first at ten or twelve weeks, depending on the nature of the temporary shot. The permanent or adult shots immunize the pup against distemper, hepatitis, and leptospirosis, all of which are deadly. The cost is $9 per shot, or a total of $18. The word *permanent* is slightly misleading, since the permanence lasts for only one year. Thus:

3. Booster shot. This is given annually and on the anniversary, a few days more or less, of the last permanent shot. It continues the immunity for another year, costs $9 and is worth it, especially for any dog who comes in contact with other dogs or dog owners.

Of the above, the average purchased pup will only need the permanents. At six or seven months, she may need a rabies shot. If so, the shot is another $9 and usually it's good for two years.

4. Worming. Despite contrary opinions by self-appointed experts, just about every pup whelped anywhere in the world comes equipped with worms and needs help to become unequipped. Worms are not optional; they are there; they reoccur, and every dog should be wormed twice a year. The canine can be host

to several different types of worms, and it always helps to know which ones are present. When the dog is entertaining hookworms, it really is silly to treat him for roundworms. To identify the worm, supply the vet with a recent stool and let him use his microscope and supply the proper pills. Worming at home, under a vet's direction, is very simple these days. The cost is under $5.

And then there is heartworm. Once restricted to southern climes, this worm has now spread just about everywhere in North America and is only rare where mosquitoes are rare. More than sixty known species of the little buzzer carry the larvae, deposit them on the dog's skin while biting the animal, then fly away to find another victim. The larvae they leave behind are better known as *microfilariae*, and the tiny micros somehow work under the skin, find the bloodstream, and ride along until they mature into heartworms. They eventually block the flow of blood and kill the dog.

If you live in mosquito country part of the year or all of the time, your pooch needs heartworm prevention on a daily basis or for that period of the year prescribed by your vet. Only a vet can provide you with the medication, in pill, powder, or liquid form. I prefer the liquid form, since it can be mixed in with the daily meal, and the diner never knows. I buy it by the gallon and the monthly per dog cost is about one dollar.

Since it is impossible to predict unexpected illnesses and accidents, there's no way to estimate annual vet costs for a pup. Currently, a pup of mine gets everything mentioned above (except for the booster shot), so vet expenses for the first year run to a minimum of fifty dollars. With luck, the bill won't run as much as that the next, or any other year.

The fifty-dollar first-year figure does not include *neutering*, the polite term for spaying a bitch or castrating a male. Either way, polite or specific, the term relates to a safe surgical procedure that guarantees the impossibility of parenthood for the canine patient. Neutering does not endanger the health or longevity of a pooch. It is always a good idea in the case of mongrels, since there are enough unwanted pups crowding the humane shelters and wandering over the landscape. And it is also a good idea in the case of purebreds whose owners do not plan on breeding or showing.

Neutering is an added expense, and although it's optional, it's worth the money in the long run. The best age for surgery has not been determined, and vets vary in their opinions that it is from six months to a couple of years. Most dog owners who opt for neutering think that ten to twelve months is about right. At that age range, my vet charges $50 for spaying and about half that for castrating. The sums include a couple of days of hospitalization, just to safeguard against infection. Recuperation is quite rapid.

Low-cost neutering clinics are now sponsored in a growing number of communities, and charges there are always considerably under those of local vets. The vets don't mind, since the clinics are designed for those dog owners who otherwise couldn't afford the operation. While there may never be enough low-cost clinics to keep the canine surplus of homeless dogs from diminishing, they could keep that surplus from expanding. In any event, they do reflect the growing concern of responsible dog owners who have no interest in breeding. Today, better than forty percent of owned bitches are neutered, and that's a healthy 25 percent more than males. Obviously, owners of males aren't too interested in control. Chauvinists are deeply offended at the mere thought of neutering their dogs.

While food and vet expenses aren't the only costs incurred by dog owners, they are usually the major ones, and together they represent the basic overhead for the average dog. In the case of a fifty-pounder, the dog's first year cost should run to about $275, and every year thereafter about $100 less—assuming, of course, that the dog doesn't suffer any accidents requiring the attention of a vet. The expenses for a smaller dog will run under those figures and for a heavier dog will top them.

In the dollars-and-cents category, there are always such minor items as annual license fee, collar and leash, nail clipper, brush and comb, whistle, and the like, each costing less than you'd charge a neighbor for mowing the lawn. And then, if money is the least of your problems and common sense doesn't run in your family, you are free to invest a tidy sum in such impractical doodads as a mink coat or a raincoat, booties and sunglasses, fancy beds and pillows, crazy toys and impossible-to-forget perfumes, and a countless array of other doggy items all designed to please your vanity, not to make life easier for your dog. If you go in for those things, some people will accuse you of spoiling your beast. If so, look at it this way: if any of these expensive gifts are chewable, your dog will chew them. Sooner or later, that is. But whenever, it's always better to have him or her chew the useless than destroy the legs of your mother's Louis IV chairs.

The major pleasure that is derived from dog ownership is companionship of an agreeable nature. If you believe (and please do) what you have already read on these pages, then you will extend yourself and be rewarded—not overnight, but sooner than you think—with a lasting measure of your dog's devotion, loyalty and obedience. And when that great day comes, you'll wonder why it took you so long to actually own a dog and how you ever got along without one: a friend in need when you need one, a sympathetic listener when your private world turns sour, an eager celebrant when you're walking tall, and always a comfort during the lonely hours.

This remarkable animal comes into the world as helpless, fearless and innocent as a human baby, but develops at a much faster pace. At seven weeks, the average pup is a veteran at seeing, hearing and smelling, doesn't need mama, and is just beginning to think. Those simple thoughts—most of them concerned with eating and fun and games—have plenty of room to float around in his or her almost adult-sized brain. As the weeks roll by, the pup's intelligence increases by leaps and bounds. Not that it matters, but on an intellectual level, a ten-month-old pup is a genius compared to a baby of the same age, and the pup is also far more capable.

Canine intelligence is tops among domestic animals, and hardly anyone but dedicated cat lovers disagrees. Still, it's nothing much compared to human intelligence, although it is constantly over-rated by those who are impressed by the dog's other capabilities. Although the dog comes up short in intellect when compared to humans, the average canine is long on instincts and senses, and superior to people in most of them. Because of their pushed-in faces, such breeds as the Pug, Boxer and Bulldog are minor league when it comes to trailing and tracking, but even their modest scenting powers are vastly superior to any person's. If healthy, any dog's hearing is also keener than ours, and pound for pound, they're easily tops in strength, stamina and speed, unless the breed was specifically developed by humans for slowness.

And then there is vision. Whether a dog's eyes are superior to ours is debatable and a matter of personal opinion. Dogs are color-blind and live in a world of blacks and whites and grays, and while that might seem like a disadvantage, many television addicts don't think so. Otherwise, dogs' sight is on a par with ours when looking straight ahead, but, because their eyes are wide-set, their peripheral vision has more range and they can glance to the rear with a slight turn of the head. Those eyes also have another big advantage that ours lack: a third lid. When danger threatens, this lid instantly slides over the eye. It is usually blood red, sometimes pink, and seeing it for the first time can really startle a person.

As if to demonstrate the fact that superior instincts and senses aren't everything, a healthy pup and most of his or her elders eat and eat as if there's no tomorrow and until the food runs out. Because so many loving owners love unwisely when it comes to feeding their pets, overweight canines are the rule rather than the exception both in this country and in Canada.

Up ahead, we'll learn why this is a very dangerous state of

affairs for any pup. Here and now it is enough to know that the canine's uncontrollable appetite is regarded as a sure sign of limited intelligence by such deep thinkers as animal behaviorists and ailurophiles (otherwise known as cat fanciers). Those critics claim that the average kitten knows when to stop and won't overeat.

They are right. Of course, many of the critics themselves are obese.

# 2

# About the Breeds

The world of dogs is currently populated by more than four hundred established pure breeds and an infinite variety of mixed breeds. About half of the pure breeds are now in residence in North America although not all are recognized by the American Kennel Club (AKC) or the Canadian Kennel Club (CKC). About fifty are found in very small numbers and classified as rare. While there's no way of counting the different varieties of mongrels present on this side of the Atlantic, there are more varieties in the United States alone than there are pure breeds in the world, to put it mildly.

While nature had a hand in the process, people are responsible for the evolution of every pure breed, and each of today's breeds is the end result of breeds that were established earlier. The ancestors of those earlier breeds remain unknown in some cases, but that doesn't alter the fact that dedicated people were behind every pure breed and that the method they employed was selective breeding. The selective breeders were always dreamers, in that they dreamed of producing a better breed of dog for a certain purpose (herding, hauling, ratting, trailing, retrieving, guarding), and with desired coat, color, size and temperament.

These days canine authorities feel we have too many pure breeds, but that hasn't stopped the dreamers, and several new breeds are in the final stages of development right now. The most recent, and thus youngest, of the pure breeds is the Wolf-Chow Dog, recognized by the German Canine Association (1975) and other ruling bodies of dogdom. Now more than ten generations old, the breed is a cross of the Chow Chow and the German Wolfspitz, and is not an immediate offspring of an unfriendly wolf. If any representatives of the new breed have reached this country, they aren't barking and remain unreported.

None of the pure breeds recommended here are that new; indeed, most have been around and pleasing owners for more than a century. The big advantage in selecting a purebred pup is that he or she is a known quantity, in the sense that you can look into the future and visualize what the dog is going to be like. You can usually be pretty sure of the eventual size, type of coat and color, and other specifications typical of the breed. And you can be almost sure that the breed temperament will be true, so long as the breeder knows what he or she is doing. However, your hope that the pup will not develop physical defects is a gamble if you buy from an irresponsible breeder or a pet store, since many weaknesses are inherited.

The continuing and growing popularity of the purebreds is based on three major predictables: size, characteristics, and temperament. Since this is true, one has every right to wonder why the mongrel is still so popular. One of the biggest reasons is the widely held belief that the average mongrel is healthier, more intelligent and easier to train than the average purebred. Poppycock! Sure, there are outstanding mongrels and yes, bum purebreds come by the bushel, especially in the very popular breeds. But whereas the average purebred pup is predictable, the same cannot be said of a juvenile mongrel. While both are the end results of inherited factors, usually nothing is known about a given mongrel pup's sire and grandparents, and all of the other dogs in the family tree.

But even though the mongrel pup is always a risk, enough good ones come along to keep the mixed bloods in vogue. Those good ones are around by the tens of thousands, and all are great pets and people lovers, and some have been trained to perform certain duties. Along with all the pure breeds, mongrels belong to the family *Canidae*.* That scientific fact, despite the popularity of mongrels, has not until now won them any formal recognition. Readers are here invited to share the honor of giving them a breed name. Let them be known in all their disguises (sizes, coats, tails) as the *Americanis*. With luck, it is possible to select an Americanis pup who will be friendly and lovable and suitable for any social occasion that is not hosted by the American Kennel Club.

One shouldn't need much luck to find that same personality in a purebred pooch. Granted that their breeding has been rational, Collie pups are friendly, happy and willing to learn. Unless an owner makes a career out of mistreating dogs, a good Collie is always a pleasure to own. Ah, there's the rub. The Collie has been a very popular breed for over a century, and breed popularity is seldom any help to traditional personality, appearance and health.

As surely as night follows day, average breed quality is sure to decline as popularity ascends. It was ever thus and always will be, and the fault is human rather than canine. Since one of the parallel effects of a breed's popularity is a growing demand for pups of the breed, supplying pups to help meet that demand becomes irresistible for those owners who figure it's an easy way to put money in the bank. So they become breeders.

Every year a healthy percentage of these new Collie breeders turns out to be composed of lovely, intelligent people who have been too busy to research the dogs they mate and are themselves afflicted by *kennel blindness*, the dog game's term for a dog owner whose love for his or her beast blinds the person to that loved one's obvious defects. Since first-grade pups are rarely

---

*The domesticated dog is just one member of the family. The others include the wolf, fox, jackal, dingo and hyena.

produced by second-grade parents, kennel-blind breeders have not helped the Collie. The same can be said for a couple of dozen other breeds. At this time in American history, it requires more than luck and cash to find a quality pup in any of our first twenty-five popular breeds.

When a breed attracts too many careless breeders, the first hallmark of the breed to go down the drain is *temperament*, better known as the personality that made the breed famous in the first place. Today the woods are full of beautiful Shetland Sheepdogs who tremble in the presence of a butterfly, noble-looking Doberman Pinschers who prefer chewing human legs to old shoes, and nervous-Nellie Poodles who wet the rug when the telephone rings. They are the results of foolish breeding and make very unsatisfactory pets. As pups, of course, their price tags are the same as those for pups who are carefully bred and worth the money.

Still, it isn't difficult to find a good pup in the breed of your choice, so long as you are not in a great hurry to acquire a canine pal. While you might find the right pup tomorrow, a search of weeks is more likely, and it always helps if you can enlist the help of a veteran dog fancier who has friends active in your breed. The veteran won't be able to lower the asking price for pups, but he or she should be able to recommend reputable breeders. This will lessen the risk. To obliterate the risk factor, of course, it will help to remember a healthy portion of the inside information found on these pages. Sometimes, even in the very best of properly bred litters, your heart will go out to a pup who really isn't worth taking home.

The shy pup is an example. Shyness is found in all pure breeds and in the Americanis. It is more prevalent in some breeds; it comes in both sexes, and it is the least desirable canine trait known to humanity. In a mild case, the pup is timid to the extent that he or she is suspicious of anything or anybody new and spooked by just about any sound except that of his or her master's voice. In a severe case, the canine develops into a fear-biter, a destroyer of valuable articles, and a dog not trustworthy in personal habits.

Mild, severe or in between, shyness is usually inherited, and while it can skip a generation, it seldom skips two. Thus, inherited shyness is almost always handed down from a pup's sire or dam or both, or from one or more of the grandparents. A pup with the quirk will demonstrate it by the time he or she is eight weeks old and might be the only shy member in a litter. It doesn't take any special talent to spot such a pup, but sometimes it's tough for a sentamentalist ("Poor puppy, he needs me") to refrain from buying one.

And then there is *kennel shyness*, also known as *induced* or *environmental*. The pup is not born with the malady, but develops it because of living conditions during the early weeks or after going to the new home. Even if a pup is bold at eight weeks, she can go to her new home and be shy at twelve weeks if she is not given enough human companionship. An example would be a normal pup whose new home is an exclusive kennel and run, but the pup hardly ever sees her master when it isn't meal or cleanup time. The more the pup lacks socialization, the faster the timidity develops, and the rule holds true whether the new home is a kennel, a dog house to which she's tied, a pen in a garage, or a room in a house. She just isn't old enough to be alone most of the time.

Canine shyness, inherited or induced, cannot be cured. Sufficient amounts of companionship, sympathetic care and training and patience will lessen the trait, but it will never go away. Sometimes it seems that it will, as in the case of a pup who has been brought along very carefully and is much less shy at ten months than he was at three months. But shyness never goes away entirely. At one year of age, a dog's degree of shyness is there to stay and prayers won't help.

When you are selecting a pup from a well-bred litter, it's wise to put your own judgment on the line as to whether the one you like is shy. A good pup is always outgoing and demonstrates this by being curious and bold, playful and aggressive. A shy one avoids games and friendly hands and often retreats to the farthest corner as the breeder explains, "That one is always looking for something. A real explorer." Breeders defend their canine products with the zeal of used-car salesmen, and asking if a pup is shy is a sure route to instant dislike.

There are many myths about shyness, and one of the most popular concerns sex: a bitch pup is more likely to be shy or to turn shy at some future date. This refers to inherited shyness, of course, and it is pure baloney. The genes that produce canine self-distrust do not discriminate as to sex. Often the smallest pup in a litter is a bold bitch and the biggest, strongest male pup is afraid of his own shadow. She, of course, is the logical pet choice.

Old-timers in the dog game will tell you that she'd still be the best bet even if her bigger brother were bold and not filled with fear. I agree. I've bred, raised, trained, observed and supported a sufficient number of pups to convince myself and anyone who will listen that, all things being equal except sex, a female pup is a wiser choice as an all-around pet. She's easier to train and the training can start earlier. She also matures more rapidly than her litter brothers, and as an adult, she's less likely to wander away from home in search of adventure. And in most breeds most of the time, for reasons that have never really made sense, female pups wear lower price tags than their litter mates of the opposite sex.

Nonetheless, most first-time dog owners opt for a male pup. This has been going on ever since the first purebreds arrived on these shores, and as American traditions go, it is one of our most irrational. The basic reason has been, and continues to be, the single word *oestrum*, the time of passion for the female dog that is commonly known as heat period or season. Under any name, it amounts to a span of about three weeks during which a prime time occurs when the bitch will accept the advances of a male and can be bred. Prime time usually runs for a week, give or take a few days.

A bitch pup comes into her first season some time after she's six months old, but seldom later than her tenth month. After that, if she's healthy, the average bitch comes into season again every six months, although every four months and every twelve months are not uncommon cycles. Whatever her schedule, it remains constant throughout the bitch's good years and into her old age. Whenever she's in season, the bitch discharges droplets of pinkish or reddish fluid. The droplets are frequent but not continuous, as in the case of a leaky faucet.

If she's a house pet and kept in the house, a bitch in season is not ideal for a fussy owner who thinks it would be cruel to confine her to one room. Nor, until now, has she been ideal for the careless owner, since a bitch in her prime time will try every trick in the book to escape and find a mate. For the fussy and the careless and everybody else, the obvious, easy answer has always been spaying the bitch. But people have scores of foolish reasons for objecting to this safe surgery, two of the most prevalent being "She won't lead a happy life" and "But what if I change my mind and want to breed her?"

To the first, rubbish. To the second, happy news: at this writing, a contraceptive dog food is waiting in the wings and ready to go. It's been tested, it's safe, and it has no side effects. Fed to any bitch as a steady diet, it will prevent her from coming into season. Remove her from this special diet and she will, in due course, come into season. If it is not already on your supermarket shelves, it will be soon, and it will be competitively priced. Prescription will not be necessary.

As your circle of dog lovers widens, you can be sure that you'll run into people who once owned a bitch and loved her very much and brag about her talents, but now say, "Never again." They'll tell you that her seasons were neither an inconvenience nor a problem, for they had been wise enough to construct an outdoor shelter and run for her, and the accommodations were spacious, comfortable and escape proof. The trouble came from romantic males owned by other people. Sooner or later, the breezes carried the seasonal scent of the bitch to every dog in a five-mile range, and those dogs (if not confined) hurried to her yard and filled the days and nights with the sounds of their howls and fights. And they ruined shrubbery, chased cats, dirtied steps and walks and made life miserable in other ways for neighbors on each side of the bitch's owner, to say nothing of her owner.

Well, scenes like that don't have to occur anymore. Thanks to the contraceptive dog food, it's now possible to own a bitch and enjoy all her pet virtues while minimizing her one potential disadvantage. When word gets around, maybe her price tag will be the same as her litter brothers'. Three cheers for Bitch's Lib.

# 3

# The Best Breeds for Young Dog Lovers

The world of the canine, as interpreted by humans, is always oversupplied with theories and truths. Few are absolute, but it's pretty close to the complete truth to say that the more we learn about dogs, the more we realize there's much more to learn. It is also true to say that very few unimpeachable dog fanciers—those with at least twenty active years in the dog game—will agree with all of the pure breeds recommended herein.

This is understandable. It does hurt to have a favorite pure breed left out in the cold, particularly when the fancier can identify numerous dogs of the breed who were and are angels with young people as well as old people, strangers and bandits. The fact is that every pure breed on earth can boast of such angels—those dearly beloved beasts who would not offend a baby, flea or sidewalk. Unfortunately, those angels are often in the minority.

Of the many breeds that are not included on our Best Breeds list, some missed by a questionable whisker, and through no fault of their own. For inclusion on the list, a breed had to pass these tests:

**Availability.** Pups of the breed must be reasonably easy to find in North America. Thus, the Spinone Italiano, a US resident for about fifty years and a worthy candidate, is not present.

**Breeders.** A very high percentage of reliable breeders should exist. Every pure breed has nitwit breeders, but a few have too many.

**Soundness.** A reliable breeder does the utmost to prevent the recurrence of inherited defects, such as hip dysplasia (see page 103) and progressive retinal atrophy. The risks are still major in some breeds.

**Temperament.** A compatible, easygoing, responsive personality amounts to good temperament, and responsible breeders preserve this by culling any brutes and shy misfits from breeding stock. To some unknown but important degree, it has been impossible to completely eradicate undesirable instincts in some breeds. Thus, if a breed was originally developed for attack work, there's always the chance, however slim, that the instinct or trait will surface in a living member of the breed, given the right conditions. Such a breed is therefore not recommended.

**Size.** Some like 'em big, some like 'em small; and then there are the Group V breeds, or the toys, These tiniest of the pure breeds—even those who pass the other tests—are not sturdy enough for our Best Breeds list. Developed long ago as lap dogs for upper-class adults, today's toys are better suited for adults (any class) who constantly watch where they step. Toys do not have strong backs.

Well, that's how a Best Breeds list is whelped. This one, anyway. While I take full responsibility for the selection of the pure breeds, much of the deepest thinking was done by others. All are veteran dog fanciers who live in America, and all are breeders, past or present; some are also breed judges, and each is recognized as a canine authority. By agreement, the names of these members of the jury are not acknowledged here.

Eighteen authorities were asked to name twenty-five pure breeds as the best for young dog-lovers, basing their choices on the five tests. My own twenty-five choices were added, and a grand total of sixty-four breeds was noted. Of these, some were mentioned on every list, others on most, and still others on just one or two.

The original intent had been to make up a list of twenty-five pure breeds, basing the selections on the number of times a given breed had been mentioned. It seemed simple enough, but there were too many unexpected ties, and the final list—in fairness to all the tie-makers and their supporters—grew to thirty-eight pure breeds. The Americanis, an added starter, represents the sentimental choice of author and editor, and will come as a surprise to the cooperating authorities, the AKC, the CKC, and dog fanciers all over the world. But you can't argue with millions of pure dogs, even if they don't happen to be purely bred.

With only a couple of exceptions, the thirty-eight purebreed finalists are recognized by either or both the AKC and the CKC, as will be noted in the parenthesis following each breed's name. The breeds appear by group and in alphabetical order. They have not been rated and are regarded as equals under the sun. For all the breeds recognized, by the AKC and the CKC—including those that didn't make the list—see Chapter Nine.

Overall, the Best Breeds list offers a generous range of sizes, weights, coats, colors and general appearances. You really can't go wrong on any one of them, although several (as noted) will be happier living outside city limits.

# GROUP 1: SPORTING DOGS
## Clumber Spaniel (AKC, CKC)

It's fair to say that these dogs are making a strong comeback in the land where they were once big favorites. The Clumbers' heyday in America was just about a century ago, when game birds and fowl were so abundant that hunters had a hard time missing shots. Speed was not essential, and Clumbers proved to be ideal for flushing and retrieving shot game. They could work their way through heavy cover, slog through a swamp and battle wild waves. Slow, steady workers, their popularity slid downhill as other, flashier sporting breeds caught the imagination of the sporting gentry.

The breed was developed in France around 1700, arrived in England in 1840, and finally reached the U.S. in 1870. Breeding declined in a hurry after 1890 in all three countries, and for a while it looked as though the Clumber would not survive the First World War. Fortunately, several breeders in England managed to keep the breed going, and finally around 1950, interest was revived in this country.

Clumbers will run all day, but they won't win any races. Among their virtues are patience, willingness and devotion. The body— long, low and stocky—isn't designed for jumping, so unguarded dinners on the table are reasonably safe. An average male stands eighteen inches and weighs fifty-five pounds, or one inch and ten pounds more than an average bitch.

For show purposes, the tail must be docked short and the silky coat should be dense, straight and on the long side. White with lemon or orange are the proper colors, and that means mostly white with the lemon (or orange) pretty solid on the ears, ticked on the muzzle and legs, and evenly marked on the head. Because of all the white, the Clumber coat is not ideal for the city. Coat care, combing and brushing are not a problem away from municipal soot and grime.

The Clumber is the heaviest of the many spaniel breeds and also the least noisy and excitable—something to remember if there are small fry in the family who think that a dog is a pony.

Overall, the Clumber is an easygoing, engaging dog who still retains the old hunting instinct, but isn't used much in the field these days. There's no way to hurry the beast. If you've never seen one, don't despair, but don't ask a member of your local fish and game club. Go to a dog show instead.

## English Setter (AKC, CKC)

There are almost a score of setter breeds—most European countries developed at least one—but only a trio have flourished on this side of the Atlantic. Of these, English Setters are probably, the best known, and should be: they've been here since about 1872, and some of our leading canine historians insist that they are the world's oldest gundogs. The belief is that the English Setters were breeding true as early as 1350, but the documented fact is that the dogs, as we more or less know them today, had their beginnings in the 1850s. Within a decade, they were big favorites in their native England, and a decade or so later they began achieving amazing popularity here. Sportsmen liked their field instincts, dog fanciers found their beauty irresistible and dog lovers put them high on the list as pets.

With a few dips now and again, that early popularity has continued, but along the way the breeders split into three camps: some bred for field, some for show and some for pet-and-show. Often, many generations of field stock produce great hunters who don't look much like the breed standard, while overbreeding for show has resulted in dogs of refined beauty and little substance. The pet-and-show breeder is the one to look for, since his or her pups are more likely to be sound in body, and at least average in beauty, and to display the famous English Setter affection.

English Setters make great pals, but they also like company to an abnormal canine degree. They resent being alone, and that can be a drawback, but fortunately they will accept another dog (and sometimes a cat) as a social equal and not sulk for too long—a very forgiving nature.

Aside from requiring plenty of attention, their other basic need is daily exercise, and that doesn't make them good candidates for city life. The same can be said of all the other sporting breeds.

This breed's long coat requires a little grooming on an almost daily basis, and a coarse comb and stiff brush do the trick. Black and white and the same plus tan are the two best-known coat colors, but there are numerous permissible color combinations (such as lemon, orange, liver and the beltons*), and there's nothing wrong with solid white. Markings are unimportant, but heavy patches of color on the body don't help for show.

Give or take a little, males stand twenty-five inches and tip the scales at sixty-five pounds; as is usual in most breeds, bitches are a little less on both counts. As adults, both sexes look long in body, but that's because of the coat and natural tail. Ratio of length to height is only 11:10. That is, they are only a little longer than they are tall. Field dogs often come a lot smaller, and a haughty dog fancier refers to them as Swamp Setters.

## English Springer Spaniel (AKC, CKC)

Another old-timer. So old that they were around before anybody thought of inventing the shotgun, but just how old remains a mystery. There's nothing unusual about this, and it also applies to many other pure breeds that were established by 1850. Prior to that date, very few breeders kept complete records. Thus the histories of the senior breeds amount to a blend of many sources: correspondence, diaries, a few published works, art and tales handed down from generation to generation.

Since it all happened this side of 1850, we can be very sure that the English Springer Spaniels are the immediate ancestors of English Cocker Spaniels, and that they sired American Cocker Spaniels, who have long been too popular for their own good. In hunting parlance, all three are known as land breeds, but English Springers are equally adept on water retrieves.

English Springers are among the easiest purebreds to housebreak and train, granting that the owner is neither lazy nor an idiot. Happy dogs, they're eager to please, good mixers, like plenty of action, and Endurance is their middle name. Over the last twenty-five years, American breeders have paid particular

---

*For this and any other terms you might find confusing, consult the Glossary.

attention to type, and today's pet, show and field dogs are look-alikes.

A dislike for confinement and a craving for action make these dogs very poor bets for city life. Their medium-length coats, flat or wavy, need no special care, but a little daily grooming is always a good idea. The long ears should be checked out after a swim or a run through a field. Keep the interiors dry and clean to prevent the coming of infections and vet's bills. Black, white, liver and tan are the colors, either as combinations or roans, but never alone.

Like most members of the Spaniel family, English Springers sport docked tails. They have solid, short-coupled bodies, or 10:10 ratio. The ideal size for a male is twenty inches at the withers and fifty pounds—just right for this long-striding, smooth-moving beauty.

## Flat-Coated Retriever (AKC, CKC)

Ancestry unknown. According to rumors, other retrievers, setters and maybe collies are behind this breed. And then there are these facts: (1) Flatcos are native to England, where they first came to popular attention about 1860 and went on to receive great acclaim at shows, on land and water, and in the home; (2) around 1890, they were the most popular sporting dogs in both England and America; and (3) they lost the top spot over there in 1915 and here in 1900, and never recouped in either country, as other pure breeds came along and dominated the attention of dog lovers.

The good news is that interest in Flatcos has been stirring on both sides of the Atlantic, and the best breeding is now found on this side. These handsome dogs are seldom seen trotting down the street, but they are appearing in greater numbers at dog shows, and that's where to see them, harvest first hand information and judge for yourself. A dog lover has to be very unlucky to go wrong with this breed—or live in the heart of a city.

Flatcos are hardy, sensible and reasonably quiet. They get

along well with people, have been known to charm dog haters, and are called delightful by appreciative owners. They require a little more discipline than other dogs of this size, but what they learn as pups is remembered for life—if the memory isn't too unpleasant. All through life, they dote on exercise.

In body, these dogs are a little long to be called short-coupled, and the coat and feathered, natural tail lend a false impression of more length.

The coat is dense, quite fine in texture, and of medium length. It's straight, lies flat and is always either a solid black or a solid liver. Yellow pups occur infrequently; the color disqualifies them for show, but it's okay for Obedience. Whatever the coat color, grooming is fairly simple. Just give the coat a workout with a hard-bristled brush about once a week.

An average male will go twenty-four inches and sixty-five pounds and looks something like a streamlined Labrador in the wrong coat.

## German Shorthaired Pointer (AKC, CKC)

The class of the world's many pointing breeds, German Short-hairs are also among the youngest (1870), and their German breeders were no better than the British at keeping records. Still, historians have come up with fragmentary evidence that indicates that other pointers and hounds are in their family tree. Whatever their ancient history, German Shorthairs have been card-carrying canines at the AKC since 1930, and have proved so satisfactory on birds and as house pets that they're getting almost too popular for their own good. Still, the reliable breeders outnumber the crazies, and good pups can be found from coast to coast.

The average German Shorthair has energy to spare and is not the best dog around for apartment living or for anyone who prefers the boob tube to fun and games. Confined to an outdoor kennel, they are rarely quiet and fill the night with the kind of music that keeps light sleepers unhappy. In one's home, however, this dog—depending on sex—makes a perfect lady or gentleman canine.

The breed features a clean-cut head up front, a short back and powerful quarters (with docked tail) to the rear. The coat is dense, short and harsh to the touch, and a cinch to groom. Solid liver is okay, and so are any combinations of liver and white. That white is always grayish, not chalky. For show, not even a touch of black is permissible.

Males stand twenty-four to twenty-six inches at the withers, and the biggest weigh about seventy pounds. Smaller sizes seem to predominate.

And then there are the less-known German Wirehaired Pointers (AKC, CKC). While similar, they are not a variety of the German Shorthaired Pointers but a separate and younger breed developed in this century by sportsmen who figured that a wire coat would provide more protection in heavy cover. Aside from coat, the difference between the two breeds is insignificant, and the German Wirehaired Pointer is also a good bet if you're lucky enough to find one.

## Golden Retriever (AKC, CKC)

One of the world's most beautiful breeds, these natives of Great Britain were unknown on these shores prior to 1900, and they are among the very few pure breeds to be introduced via the West Coast (British Columbia, in particular). Goldens were breeding true by 1860, but their ancestry was a matter of wild speculation for almost a hundred years. Then, to the surprise of even well-educated canine historians, the records of the original breeder came to light. Just as so many breed lovers thought, at least one earlier retriever and a couple of water spaniels are in the Golden's family tree. The original breeder didn't specify those breeds, and they may not have been established pure breeds.

During their first three decades in America, Goldens developed into very popular sporting dogs. They were great in the field and wonderful in the home—sportsmen liked them, and their wives and children loved them. Then Labradors arrived on the scene, dominated the field trials, won the admiration of sporting people and stole the show.

Today, Goldens are seen more at dog shows than in the field, and their pet rating equals that of any other sporting breed. Quality pups are very willing to learn and thus easy to train, and proof of that is the number of Goldens found in Obedience as well as the many used as guide dogs for the blind.

The dog's body is built for action and durability. The ratio of length to height is a little long (12:11). The Golden always carries topcoat and should carry a very short, dense undercoat (but this has been lost in some bloodlines). The topcoat is of medium length and lies flat, either straight or wavy, and is fairly water repellent. Occasional combing, at least weekly, keeps the coat in shape.

The name *Golden* comes from coat color, of course. In England, this means a yellow of any shade from cream to mahogany. Over here, the breed standard calls for "lustrous gold," or in between cream and mahogany, but that doesn't keep cream- or mahogany-coated dogs from winning at the shows. If a judge decides that cream is really lustrous gold, so be it.

Pups are often lighter in coat than they will be as adults. The yellow shade on the ears is darker and close to the mature shade of the body—something to remember if you worry about proper color on a pup. The other thing to remember is size, but only if you intend to show your Golden. Dogs are disqualified if they stand above or below these ranges: males, 20–25 inches; bitches, 20½–23½ inches. At 24 inches, a Golden should weigh about sixty-five pounds.

# Gordon Setter (AKC, CKC)

Gordon Setters are natives of Scotland, where they were

breeding true by 1620. That makes them older than the English and Irish Setters and possible ancestors of both. They were the first of the setter breeds to arrive in America, but despite that head start, they have never achieved the popularity of the others, and there's not much chance that they ever will. Setter lovers consider the Irish much more beautiful and the English a little more beautiful. That seems to be the only rationale for the fact that Gordons aren't better known.

But beauty isn't everything, and these dogs have a lot going for them under their black and tan coat colors. The average beast of the breed is very responsive to training, grows like a weed and requires more exercise than can be found in a city, unless the master owns an abandoned racetrack. He's known as a one-family dog, is loyal to those he knows and wary of strangers without being a threat. His one drawback as a house pet could be a tendency to resent another canine under the same roof. This dog usually wants total affection.

Since Gordons have not been overbred, their field instincts are reasonably sharp. That, of course, makes them the best choice among setters for the person who hunts occasionally and wants the services of a dog, but not the expense involved with a professionally trained bird dog. The Gordon Setter ranges fairly close, won't run over the hill and out of sight and is willing to get his or her feet wet.

A proper Gordon Setter's body is almost short-coupled, or not quite as long as an English Setter's. On the other hand, the Gordon is sturdier and carries more leg bone. The coat is always black with tan markings, although the breed standard approves of a very small white spot on the chest. The coat is long and soft, lies straight or a little wavy and should not be curly. If not really beautiful, this dog is certainly handsome.

Sometimes, in a litter of otherwise perfectly marked pups, there will be a solid red pup or one who is predominately tan or buff. Those exceptions are okay as pets and eligible for Obedience, but not for show.

The average male stands twenty-six inches and weighs about seventy-five pounds. Linebred Gordon Setter litters are often sold out before they're whelped, so reserving a pup in advance is usually a good idea.

## Irish Water Spaniel (AKC, CKC)

The tallest of the spaniel breeds, Irish Water Spaniels are not as well known as most of their shorter cousins, although they were both popular and appreciated a hundred years ago when wildfowl was abundant and American market hunters needed water retrievers who would perform in any weather. As we know them today, Irish Water Spaniels were breeding true by 1850, so the Irish were aware of the breed's talents decades before us.

The records show that Justin McCarthy of Dublin developed the final, still-current version of this spaniel from two earlier varieties. McCarthy began his selective-breeding program in 1822, so it took him almost thirty years before he was sure of his results. Little else is known about the breed, although a few canine historians now speculate that one side of the Irish Water family tree might go all the way back to 1588, when the Portuguese Water Dog may have been introduced to Ireland, more or less by accident.

Among spaniel breeds, and among all other pure breeds known or believed to be in North America, only the Irish Water Spaniel wears a rat tail. This is also known as a whip tail, but whatever it is called, it is natural, strange and reaches to the hocks. The first two to three inches of the tail (from the base) are covered with short curls, and the rest of the tail tapers to a fine point and is covered with very short, smooth hair. The oddball tail probably serves some useful purpose, and your guess is as good as any expert's.

Thanks to several outstanding show dogs and a few other star performers in Obedience, the Irish Water Spaniel has been receiving frequent mention in the press in recent years and is now better known than a decade ago. Still, most dog lovers object to the unique tail, as if it were illegal or immoral, and go to another breed. That's discrimination at its silliest, since it blinds the shallow thinker to the breed's many virtues: Deep in their hearts, Irish Water Spaniels are clowns. Fun lovers, they're quick to learn, ready to experiment, and will try almost anything. They're loyal, affectionate, love attention and are actors all the way. They dearly love the water, prefer swimming to running, and are good mixers with other dogs and friends of the family.

Although they are a little tall for their medium length, these dogs look sturdy rather than leggy and move in a bold, stylish manner. The double coat is always a solid liver, with the undercoat very short and dense and the topcoat a blanket of crisp, fairly short curls. One of the best water-shedding coats in the canine world, it is very quick drying and without odor. A few minutes with a steel comb once a week removes dead hairs and keeps the coat in shape.

To the rear, the rat tail is characteristic. Up front, the same can be said about the natural topknot that ends in a widow's peak. And let's not forget the smooth hair on the face and the long, curl-covered, hanging ears. It's really hard for this dog to look serious.

A big male stands twenty-four inches and weighs sixty-five pounds. It's sometimes possible to go wrong on an Irish Water Spaniel, but not very wrong. American breeding remains first-rate.

## Labrador Retriever (AKC, CKC)

The most popular of the several retriever breeds, Labs have consistently dominated their peers in field trials over the last forty-five years. They are also favorites at the shows, stars in Obedience, very dependable guide dogs for the blind, all-around performers on the farm and beloved house pets all over the world. Under their respective coats, the Lab and the Newfoundland are cousins; both are early-nineteenth-century English variations of the even earlier and long-defunct Saint John's Dog, the pride and joy of the fishing boats that sailed from Newfoundland.

Labs reached America in the 1890s but didn't attract much attention until after World War I. Then, in the 1930s and thanks to field trials, their fame zoomed, and by now everybody knows that Labs are here to stay. What everybody doesn't know is that perhaps as many as 30 percent of the pups advertised in the papers aren't worth the asking price. That's a reflection on "instant" breeders' quality, not overall breed quality. If you have a Lab pup in mind, really look around for a breeder with a good reputation.

Quality Labs have even temperaments and soft mouths, meaning that they can carry something (a duck, a Ping-Pong ball, an egg) in their jaws all day without puncturing it. Loyal to members of their human families, they sound off but don't threaten when strangers intrude, and take training in stride. On the other hand, they're usually intelligent enough to take advantage of human error, so steaks—raw or broiled—should not be left unguarded. They'll eat almost anything and have a tendency to become overweight in a hurry, so food intake should be watched.

Short-coupled, sturdily built dogs, Labs wear short, dense coats that dry quickly after a swim and seldom need grooming. If they are bred right, they also sport double coats, with the undercoat very short and soft. As for colors, the breed standard permits three, all solid: black, yellow (any shade) and chocolate (light to dark). For show, a small white spot on the chest is okay for blacks and chocolates, but, in practice, judges really don't pay much attention to patches of white. Or size, for that matter.

An average male comes close to twenty-four inches and seventy pounds. On coat color, chocolate pups are still not as abundant as blacks and yellows, but there are many more around every year.

\*    \*    \*

# Nova Scotia Duck Tolling Retriever (CKC)

Tolling dogs are trained to gambol (as does the fox by nature) on the shores of lakes and coves where wildfowl are accustomed to gather. The wildfowl become curious and drift closer to the playful dog, the better to view the beast's antics. When the ducks approach within gun range, the hunter jumps from hiding and shoots away. The fowl the hunter shoots are then retrieved by the dog. In olden days in Europe, before the gun was invented, tolling dogs lured wildfowl upstream and into nets.

The Tolling Retriever is Nova Scotia's gift to dogdom as the only pure breed ever developed there. It all happened this side of 1860, and it's reasonable to believe that the breed's family tree includes, as is claimed, both the Flat-Coated and the Labrador Retrievers, the Irish Setter (coat color) and the Rough Collie (herding instinct, tail feathering). This newcomer to the purebred scene, known herein as the Toller, is fairly well known in Canada and just getting underway in the US. To date, the breeders have maintained a high degree of quality, and it's easier to find a good Toller pup while blindfolded than in most other breeds in this chapter.

Tollers are the smallest of the retrievers found in America, but not by much, and pound for pound they're as strong and durable as any of the water specialists. If there's a living Toller who doesn't like to get his feet wet, he remains unreported, and the same cannot be said of such breeds as the Golden, Lab and Chesapeake.

An average Toller is eager to learn and thus very easy to train, especially for field work. They're friendly, spirited, love action, and would rather not be favorites on Park Avenue.

The dog is just a touch long in body, resembles a smaller edition of the Golden and also wears a double coat. The undercoat is the usual very short and woolly, while the topcoat is soft, sleek and on the long side, and lies flat. It's usually wavy down the center of the back and straight elsewhere. Fox red is the proper coat color, and if you don't know a red fox, it's almost as deep as the mahogany coat on a good Irish Setter. For show, a little white on chest or belly is permissible, but any white elsewhere is a disqualification—if the judge remembers all of the breed standard.

The average male stands a little over twenty inches and weighs forty-five to fifty pounds. There's no maximum size, but breeders hope to keep Tollers as they are, and giant dogs won't be used in breeding programs.

## Vizsla (AKC, CKC)

This is the best of the sporting breeds developed in Hungary, a superiority based on a seniority of sorts. Primitive tenth-century art and fourteenth-century manuscripts suggest that either the Viz or a very similar looking ancestor was around in olden days and used, as today, on birds, hare and other small game. And as we know them today, they're pretty much the same as they were a hundred years ago and deserve much more popularity than they currently have as family pets.

Known abroad as Hungarian Pointers, Vizslas aren't as fast in the field as other pointers—but they're fast enough. They range fairly close, and sporting people claim that their scenting power is extraordinary. As pets, these dogs retain a healthy percentage of their natural field instincts. Thus, they don't require much additional training to do an adequate job on game birds.

It's tough to find a lazy Viz. This dog is quite lively by nature and not designed for city life, unless your living room is air conditioned and the size of a school gymnasium. These are gentle, affectionate, friendly dogs, and some tend to be overprotective when it comes to family members and family possessions. They're not ugly, but they are the next best thing to a padlock. Grooming is so seldom required and so simple that further comment is unwarranted.

The short-coupled body is streamlined and much sturdier than it looks. The tail is docked long (two-thirds its natural length)—so

*Above,* English Setter, courtesy of Mrs. John Kilgus. (*Tauskey*)

*Left,* Clumber Spaniel romping in the snow is owned by the William Lloyds and E. Gies, Beau Chien Kennels, Canada.

*Below,* English Springer Spaniel, courtesy of the breeder, Mrs. Kathleen Martyn, Springcasa Kennels, Canada. *(Dale Coolidge)*

*Above,* Flat-Coated Retriever, courtesy of the owner, Vernon W. Vogel.

*Left,* Golden Retriever, courtesy of the owner, Kathy Liebler, Valhalla Farms.

*Below,* German Short-haired Pointer, courtesy of owner Irving Shaw, Dobroyd Kennels. Canada.

Gordon Setters, courtesy of the owner, Dr. T. S. Carden, Temacer Kennels. The pup is ten weeks old.

Labrador Retrievers owned by the author. The sitting pup, a chocolate, is ten months old. *(Maxine Goodwin)*

*Above,* Vizsla, courtesy of the owner, Mrs. John F. Lyons. *(Nica Lyons)*

*Left,* Irish Water Spaniel, courtesy of the owner, Arthur D. Heiny.

*Below,* Nova Scotia Duck Tolling Retriever, courtesy of the owner, Mrs. Wileen Mann, Sundrummer Kennels, British Columbia. *(Michael Carter)*

long that one wonders why it's ever docked. The breed standard calls for the docking, that's why, and it's only important for show.

The coat is smooth, very short, dense and lies close. Shedding occurs, but it's trivial. Coat color is always solid, although very small white spots on chest and feet are forgiven, making such coats almost solid. Those solid or almost solid colors range from rusty gold to any dark shade of sandy yellow. Pale yellows and cream are okay on a yellow Labrador, but not on a beast of this breed.

Males stand twenty-two to twenty-four inches, and for show a two-inch deviation either way is okay. Figure three pounds per inch, subtract six, and that's about what the dog should weigh, give or take a few ounces.

# GROUP II: HOUNDS
## Beagle (AKC, CKC)

The breed name is Middle English for *Begle*, the French name for any small hound who chased hare for the heck of it or for a living. Nobody really knows the breed's origins, but the English claim that they developed these dogs and only the Romans disagreed. Still, we can be sure that Beagles—in an assortment of sizes, but never over twenty inches—have been around in England and several European countries for some 350 years and in America for about 100 years. At one time (always abroad), there were Beagle strains so small that a couple could be carried in the pocket of a hunting coat and three were not crowded on a fat woman's lap. These "pocket" or "glove" Beagles were about the size of overweight Chihuahuas.

Contemporary Beagles reach at least twice that size and have been among America's most popular dogs for a long time. Indeed, they were *THE* most popular at one time (1953–1959) and may be again, for both pet lovers and sporting people find them hard to resist. As for the latter, there are hundreds of Beagle packs, scores of Beagle field trials, and more Beagles used by weekend hunters than all other breeds combined.

Our present concern is with Beagles as pets. The word *merry* is often used to describe them, and it refers to their spirit, not to their sadsack, houndy look. They're friendly, affectionate and playful, and can take rough-and-tumble play. And they're quite adaptable. A sensible Beagle takes the city in stride, even while questioning his or her master's choice of living site. They need daily grooming there to remove soot and grime, of course, but in suburbs or country, they take care of themselves most of the time, short of socializing with skunks.

If you are looking for a small dog, you can't go wrong on a quality Beagle. Pup prices for show and pet stock are often lower than in other pure breeds, so Beagles are a good economy buy, and future upkeep will be fairly low. Be advised that (1) finding the right breeder is important; and (2) the dogs are very social and need as much companionship, canine or human, as they can get.

This is a sturdy, short-coupled little dog who comes in two varieties for show purposes: (1) not over thirteen inches; and (2) over thirteen but not over fifteen inches. Two pounds per inch is about right.

The coat is dense, hard, close-lying and medium in length, and hound colors (white, black, tan) are appropriate. I can remember rough coats that were almost wirehaired, but that was in the 30s. Breeders have been successful in eliminating that style coat; it did not enhance breed beauty.

## Finnish Spitz (CKC)

This is the national dog of Finland, where the name is *Suomen-pystykorva*. In England and Canada, where the breed is also recognized but not as popular, the dog's nickname is Finkie. The breed was developed in the distant past as a bigger hunting dog and used on all game, but is now smaller, better balanced, and used mostly for flushing birds and small game. These days, the Finkie is regarded as a fine fit in the home, the field or the breed ring—or all three.

Pups do seem to require a little special understanding. Most are independent types and require a firm hand. That's firm as in discipline, and doesn't mean an iron hand. If canines are sensitive, count the Finnish Spitz among the leaders.

Otherwise, it's all clear sailing with this breed: friendly with you and the family, but a little wary of your friends at first. For their size, the dogs need plenty of outdoor exercise, but they settle down indoors between outings. Grooming is not a problem, and many owners claim the coat is almost self-cleaning. Maybe, but don't bet on it in the city.

Under all the coat, this is a short-coupled, agile dog who wears a bushy tail that curls up and over the back à la the Norwegian Elkhound. It's a double coat: short, dense undercoat and a fairly long topcoat that stands erect or semierect. The right color is clear fox red, also known as brownish red, and lighter shades are okay away from the body proper. For show, white is okay on the feet and as a narrow stripe on the chest.

Top size for a male is 19½ inches and about forty pounds. Although a true sporting dog, the CKC places the Finkie in the hound group. Here, the breed's lovers hope that the AKC will one day recognize the dog as proper for either the sporting or non-sporting group.

## Irish Wolfhound (AKC, CKC)

In the world of purebreds, these are the giants of them all and older than most. Their heftier ancestors date back to the glory days of Rome, and the modern version—more pleasing to the eye and a better fit in a small home—dates back to the 1880s. Irish Wolfhounds were designed to run down and bag such game as wild boar, wolf and elk, but these days they're strictly pets and show dogs, and not complaining.

Obviously, this is not the right dog for anyone who has to worry about food bills. Nor is the Wolfhound a good choice for impatient dog lovers. As if secure in the knowledge of their own brute strength, Wolfhounds cannot be forced to do anything against their will. It's always better to con them than to go in for excessive discipline.

On the bright side, they're very affectionate and loyal dogs who dote on family life and make up their own minds as to who will be their real boss. And they're great as quiet watchdogs: their size is such that they don't have to threaten in order to impress an intruder.

Pups grow at a phenomenal rate during the first seven months. A pound a day and an inch per week are not unusual during the weeks of greatest growth. After seven months, they still eat like horses, but the rate of growth slows down. Then, at eighteen months, the average Irish Wolfhound is as tall as he'll ever be, although full development often takes another year. As huge dogs go, they don't require hard exercise, although room for galloping is always healthier than a slow walk down a city street.

The coat is rough, hard, medium in length and needs a stiff brushing every few days. For show, wiry and long hair over the eyes and under the jaws is considered important. Just about any solid color (sometimes with shadings) will do, but breeders seem to prefer gray, brindle and red, with pure white and fawn not so popular.

At eighteen months, the minimum size for males is thirty-two inches and 120 pounds. They shouldn't come smaller and usually come bigger. In all the giant breeds, take-home time for pups is later than usual, and four months is about right. Pups shoot up like weeds, but overall physical development takes time.

Many naive dog lovers veto the thought of sharing their homes with an Irish Wolfhound on the grounds that the beast would accidentally make a shambles of antique furniture, lamps, plant stands, coffee tables, and objects d'art on the mantel. Let it be known that while a good Wolfhound does not step on small children or through glass doors, a tiny Yorkshire Terrier can almost destroy a china ship as a lark.

## Norwegian Elkhound (AKC, CKC)

Reliable sources insist that the deepest thinkers among our canine historians agree that the Norwegian Elkhound was running around the land now known as Norway a very long time ago. Perhaps as long ago as 5000 B.C., is the educated guess of archaeologists who have studied certain canine skeletons found in digs. If this is true, the Norwegian Elkhound is one of the wonders of nature, in that humans didn't have much of a hand, if any, in the design and development of the breed. But all theories aside, we can be very sure that over recent centuries, the Elkhound has been the friend and helper of Vikings, shepherds, farmers and hunters, and a companion for plain dog lovers.

In America, this dog remains very underrated as a pet. Many dog lovers incorrectly think they're sled dogs and would be unhappy away from snow. They'll pull a sled even without training, although they weren't designed for that purpose and would rather run down and hold at bay such beasts as bears and elk, mountain lion and raccoon. As for snow, they can take it or leave it.

This is a fine family dog. She's a good all-round pal, remarkably tolerant with impatient small fry, and eager for almost any type of activity. The adult coat dries quickly and lacks any doggy odor even when soaking wet. A few minutes with brush and comb every few days keeps the coat in top shape.

The biggest problem with an adult, if there's going to be one, concerns her poundage. While not a heavy eater, an adult Norwegian Elkhound who doesn't get sufficient exercise goes overweight in a hurry. Her master should take up jogging (with the dog).

A good Elkhound stands sturdy and four-square, the very picture of strength. She wears a double coat: light and woolly underneath, covered by a topcoat that's hard, coarse and lies close. Coat color on the body proper is always gray with black tips on the long hairs, and lighter shadings of gray elsewhere, including the underside of the curled tail. White, if any, should be hardly any.

For show, the ideal size for a male is 20½ inches and fifty-five pounds, but any size is OK for them. Reliable breeders abound. Find one.

There's also a solid black Norwegian Elkhound, but the color is not present in America. The black coat makes the dog look like an entirely different breed. Here, we recognize only the gray.

## Otter Hound (AKC, CKC)

The breed was developed some five hundred years ago and was designed, of course, for otter hunting. Hunted in packs, the Otter Hound was the pride and joy of several British kings over the centuries. However, modern times caught up with the breed: as England's rivers became more and more polluted, fewer fish survived; fish are the basic diet of otters, so the otter population dwindled; and if there are no otters to hunt, who needs an Otter Hound?

If it were not for American dog lovers, this would be a rare breed. There are now more Otter Hounds here than anywhere else, and their quality is dandy. If the Otter Hounds have been used on otter recently, somebody is keeping the news a secret, but it is not a secret that they have become beloved pets, and that they have not lost their remarkable scenting power, their love for swimming, or their durable coats.

They are good family dogs, but not for every family on the block, since they're not very good mixers and are not fond of the push-and-pull play of tiny tots. These are really one-family dogs and, surprisingly, they are catching on in the cities, as they are good-natured beasts who rate as the best shaggy dogs of their size.

The coat is reasonably waterproof, but hardly sootproof. Underneath all the coat is a heavy-set dog who is a little longer than tall (11:10), with a big head on one end and a long tail on the other. If you think shaggy hounds are unusual, consider this: the Otter Hound is the only hound (shaggy or otherwise) in America who sports webbed toes. He's also the only hound who sometimes swims underwater.

The coat is a double one: a short, woolly, almost water resistant undercoat, and a long topcoat that's hard, coarse and shouldn't run more than six inches for show. Any color or color combination is okay. A steel comb and stiff brush do for grooming, and the frequency depends on how the dog spends an average day. The more the mud or burrs, the greater the frequency.

An average Otter Hound male will stand twenty-five inches and weigh about eighty-five to ninety pounds. Some breed lovers think that the Bloodhound is in the family tree, and if you strip away the long coat, a nude Otter Hound will look quite similar to a Bloodhound. I haven't tried it.

## Scottish Deerhound (AKC, CKC)

These aristocrats of the canine world have been breeding true to form for well over two hundred years, and along the way, their admirers have not tried to change them. In many other breeds— especially since dog shows became popular—ardent admirers have actually succeeded in altering original conformations. The process is called *refinement* and is best illustrated by the mythical Boxhead Terrier. Today, a Boxhead looks something like a Dachshund, but back in 1890, the head was square, and didn't look quite right on the long body. So, through selective breeding, the dog's head was narrowed and the muzzle elongated. Any day now the very name Boxhead will be refined to Rectangularhead.

But Scottish Deerhounds have not been refined. Owners and breeders liked them as they were in days of yore, and they like them even better today. Since they haven't been changed, and they haven't been around in great numbers for a hundred years, and their breeders are first-rate, the quality of pups is very high. The contemporary Scottish Deerhound makes a noble pet for the lover of big dogs. The puppy price tag is usually on the high side, but adult Deerhounds do represent some sort of economy. They get by on less food and hard exercise than most dogs their size, and they have exceptional longevity. If there's a fat Scottish Deerhound in existence, she's hidden in her owner's garage.

Affectionate and devoted to their human families, these swift beasts are surprisingly tractable, take their lumps in stride, and wear coats that require minimum attention. "He is safe with all reasonable people, but he adores children and soon becomes their playmate and guardian," says Miss A. N. Hartley, the breed's top authority.

As giant dogs go, these are a very fine choice. And as giant dogs run, these really need and appreciate room to stretch their legs in pursuit of imaginary deer and fast spenders. However, they don't have to romp in a straight line, and a yard of half an acre will suffice for an average adult.

The Scottish Deerhound body is closer to short-coupled than it looks, and the long, strong neck (originally designed to hold back a frantic stag) is strangely graceful and hard to forget. The coat runs up to four inches in length and is harsh, dense and rather wiry over most of the body and much softer on the head, chest and belly. Coat colors are owner's choice, but light to dark grays, blue, brindles and reds seem to predominate. White is not highly regarded, and both a white blaze and a white collar disqualify for show.

A big male stands thirty-two inches and weighs in the neighborhood of 110 pounds. Whenever three dog fanciers talk about this breed, at least one is sure to remark that the Scottish Deerhound reminds him of an oversized Greyhound in a rough coat. There is, in fact, a basis for this: the Scottish Deerhound was once known in Scotland by other names, including Rough Greyhound.

Beagle, courtesy of the owner, Marcia Foy, Foyscroft Kennels. This is Ch. Kings Creek Triple Threat, one of the breed's all-time greats. (*Evelyn Shafer*)

Finnish Spitz, courtesy of the owners, Bette Isacoff and Margaret Koehler.

Norwegian Elkhound, courtesy of the owners, Dr. and Mrs. John Craige, Vin-Melca Kennels.

Irish Wolfhound, courtesy of the breeder, Jill R. Bregy.

Scottish Deerhound, courtesy of the Edward Arnolds, owner-breeders, Gwent Kennels. Photo on jacket of a sire and his five-week-old son is also from the Arnolds.

Otterhound, courtesy of the owner, Mrs. W. R. Peschka, Cragmont Kennels. (*Jayne Langdon*)

# GROUP III: WORKING DOGS
## Bearded Collie (AKC, CKC)

Another gift from Scotland, the Bearded Collie is this book's choice over the Old English Sheepdog, who is bigger, requires more grooming and food, wears an unnatural-length tail, and just might be a distant cousin. Then, too, the chances of finding a good Bearded Collie pup at a reasonable price are better. As for the other *collie* breeds, there's not much sense comparing them to the bearded pooch, since they are not related. Centuries ago, the word *collie* was Scottish for any sheepherding dog, and that's what Bearded Collies did for a living. They were used as specialists in rugged country or high up in the highlands.

The Bearded Collie population is much bigger today than it was a century ago, a remarkable fact when one considers that as recently as 1923, the breed was almost extinct, with only one breeder. She was an English woman who saved the breed and then interested other dog lovers in it, and that may be why so many Bearded Collie males are called Willis. The breed's saviour was one Mrs. G. O. Willison.

The Bearded Collie population is much bigger today than it only been on this side of the Atlantic since the early 1960s. The Canadian Kennel Club granted them full recognition in 1970, and the American Kennel Club followed suit in 1976. Now they're known from coast to coast as extremely friendly dogs, great with small fry and eager to please. They can be happy without sheep or goats and are right at home in a city apartment. Unfortunately, the coat is a natural grime collector, so grooming is a daily must in New York, Chicago, Los Angeles, Dallas and other places where people still outnumber dogs. If you live on a small farm, a Bearded Collie will herd anything from cows to chickens, and the grooming won't amount to much.

These dogs' long, lean bodies look bigger than they are because of the coat. If they're good examples, they wear a double coat: a soft, furry undercoat topped by a crop of strong, harsh and mostly flat hair. Muzzlewise, the hair is sparse on the bridge of the nose and is longer on the sides, or long enough to fall and hide the lips. Behind this, longer hairs droop chestward and form the famous beard. Coat colors, with or without white markings, include all shades of gray, black, brown, sandy and reddish fawn.

A Bearded Collie male stands twenty-one to twenty-two inches and weighs sixty to sixty-five pounds, including all that coat. A healthy member of either sex apparently does not recognize the passing of the years and remains puppy-playful into old age.

## Bernese Mountain Dog (AKC)

Four varieties of the *Sennenhunde*—"Swiss Mountain Dog" in English—are doing their thing in the Alps today. Of this quartet, only two are found in America in goodly numbers: the Bernese Mountain Dog and the Greater Swiss Mountain Dog, which is considered on following pages. These two amount to slightly different versions of a dog who was probably brought to Switzerland by the Roman legions some two thousand years ago. Over the centuries, the dog was developed a little differently in various Swiss areas. Finally, as this century dawned, the quartet of types was firm and breeding true.

Bernese Mountain Dogs were developed as jacks-of-all-trades in and around the canton of Berne. The dogs herded and guarded livestock, hauled assorted merchandise to market and served as playmates and ponies. Until somebody comes along to prove differently, it's safe to assume that the first members of the breed reached America by way of England in 1925, or just a dozen years before the American Kennel Club bestowed recognition on them.

In this country, the breed has not been put to work, but chances are that an adult Bernese will bring your cows home if you have any. The dog has never achieved much popularity, but now—at long last—about thirty breeders are in the act, more dogs are popping up at shows, and they're on their way. Most of the breeders know what they're doing, but check on OFA certification of both parents (next chapter) before buying a pup.

These are friendly beasts who don't fight discipline, are eager to learn and quite easy to train. They are good mixers, hardly ever noisy, and, for their size, don't require heavy exercise. In the East, they've been catching on in cities, proving perhaps that a dog who can take living in the Alps without an electric blanket can take living anywhere.

A Bernese is sturdy, strong, short-coupled and handsome. The coat is soft, smooth, a little wavy and on the long side, and does require simple grooming about twice a week. It's always jet black with tan markings, and for show a little white in the right places helps: on the feet and tail tip, as a blaze up the foreface, or star marking on the chest, and sparsely on the back of the neck.

The average male stands twenty-five inches and weighs sixty-five pounds. If your home situation is such that you can't keep a dog indoors, this one will be okay in an unheated kennel. Outdoors, of course, two will help keep each other warm.

## Bouvier des Flandres (AKC, CKC)

When this century began, France and Belgium were populated by a surprising variety of cattle-driving dogs. They came in all sizes, in most coats and with different ear and tail styles. Of these more-or-less pure breeds, the Boov was the only one to catch the fancy of European dog lovers, and every effort was made to standardize the breed. This was accomplished in the early 1920s. The Boov's fame spread, and a decade later he reached our shores. Here he has always been a beloved pet, and even abroad he is no longer used to drive cattle since there are better ways to get beef on the hoof from Point A to Point B.

The first of the breed to arrive in America didn't amount to much, but then the late Janet Mack, a transplanted Canadian, imported several outstanding dogs and launched the first American breeding program of any substance. For many years, her dogs—the very best in America—were happy and healthy on the Lower East Side of Manhattan. Obviously, Boovs thrived in the city before they knew the wide open spaces of America. Thus, they are proven city dogs.

Because of the increase in numbers of kooky breeders, the Boov came close to not making this preferred list. Happily, the good guys still outnumber the baddies, so here's a hearty plug for this dog—provided, of course, that you find the right breeder.

Good Boovs make great pets. They're devoted, friendly, keep a watchful eye on tiny tots, and are ready for play any time of the day. A bum Boov is stubborn, shy, and not to be trusted across the street. Finding the pups with the right temperament is the answer to all these problems. There are plenty of good ones around, so don't be conned (you can learn more about choosing a pup in the next chapter).

This dog's body is compact and powerful. The erect ears look like small triangles, and the tail is short, or about four inches. Naturally, or unnaturally in this case, the ears are cropped and the tail is docked. A good Boov always forgives the breed standard, though.

Boovs wear a double coat, with the usual soft and fine undercoat and a harsh, rough, wiry topcoat that qualifies as semishaggy or unkempt. A weekly grooming does for the pet dog, but these days a show dog is trimmed close to perfection. The mod haircuts you see at the shows can make you gasp.

Males stand twenty-five inches or so and weigh seventy pounds. If the breeding is right, a male pup is the safest choice for a peace-loving owner, as bitch pups can mature into scrappy beasties.

## Collie (AKC, CKC)

The Collie comes in one of two coats: rough and smooth. The AKC recognizes the Collie as one breed with two varieties. The CKC recognizes two distinct breeds, or Rough Collie and Smooth

Collie. Whatever your choice, each coat covers the same canine body. All clear?

In the light of coat genetics, the smooth is dominant, and that's reason enough for not breeding a Rough to a Smooth—do that often enough and there would only be Smooths in the world.

Despite the fact that the rough coat is not dominant, there are many more Roughs in the world, and that's the way it has always been. In America, the ratio of Roughs to Smooths is about eighteen to one. There really isn't any choice between the two varieties. Vote for the Rough if you want beauty and don't mind daily grooming. Go to the Smooth if you want handsomeness and minimal coat care.

A couple of centuries ago, there was more reason for choice: the Rough worked at herding and guarding sheep, and the Smooth drove the sheep to market. One for the hills, one for the roads. Here were a couple of Scottish specialists, and only Scotland's sheepherders cared.

What worries American admirers of the breed is that the Collie has been greatly refined over the past 100 years. Contemporary Collies are taller than they were in the old days, but they're not as long. The head is narrower, the stop is now quite modest, and the muzzle has been elongated. Overall, the contemporary is a svelte version of the original—among the first breeds in America—dating back to Colonial times.

Those early Collies worked for a living, whereas today's are bred for loving, showing and admiring. A worthy dog in either coat is friendly, playful, eager for companionship, fairly easy to train and, unfortunately, noisy when attention isn't sufficient.

This dog's body is a little long, rather streamlined and deep in the chest. The Rough wears a soft, closely knit undercoat, and over that is a topcoat of longish, straight, harsh hairs. The Smooth wears a hard, dense, smooth coat. Proper coat colors for both varieties are sable and white, blue merle, tricolor and white (white with markings).

The average male stands twenty-five inches and weighs

sixty-five pounds. Usually, pet-shop price tags are much higher than those of local breeders.

## Puli (AKC, CKC)

Another sheepdog, this time of Hungarian extraction and deserving of much more popularity than they've received to date, since a Puli is a much better bet for city life than those other Hungarian natives now in our midst, the Kuvasz and Komondor. The plural for Puli is not Pulis, Pulies, or Puliae. It's Pulik .

For their size, Pulik don't require a heck of a lot of exercise, but that doesn't mean they shouldn't have room to romp when in the mood. Very few have been used on sheep in this country, but they are in their element as pet and show dogs and in Obedience. The average Puli is a wary pooch, or, as the breed standard explains, "sensibly suspicious of strangers and therefore an *excellent guard.*" This means that they bark up a din when intruders approach and their noise alerts the master. Pulik will threaten but not attack, and are among the best guard dogs of that fashion in their size range.

In addition to their protective instinct, good Pulik are alert and playful, devoted and affectionate, and lovers of all the comforts found in the home. They're fine companions and fill the bill for just about everybody, the only exceptions being dog lovers who insist on leading tranquil lives and anyone who hates the thought of grooming.

The Puli is almost short-coupled and usually comes with a complete tail that curls over the back when the dog is on the alert. Occasionally a natural bobtail is whelped, and the wearer is socially acceptable. So the tail is long or bob, but never docked. Ears are also natural, V-shaped and hanging. The coat is a double, with the usual undercoat and a shaggy topcoat that is long, a little on the harsh side (never silky) and either straight, wavy, slightly curled or corded.

As for coat colors: pups come into the world as solid whites or blacks, and the former are in the minority. As the pups grow, the whites remain that way. So do some of the blacks, but others develop into rusty blacks and various shades of gray. While solid whites are okay for show, white markings on dark coats bring frowns to the brows of breed judges.

The average male stands eighteen inches, weighs just over thirty-five pounds and usually prefers what you're eating. If you own or buy a Puli, you might like to know that there is Puli blood in the Pumi, another Hungarian sheepdog who is a little smaller, not a look-alike, and hard to find in America.

## Samoyed (AKC, CKC)

It took a long time for these Siberian natives to gain their deserved popularity in America, and it's possible that their original name held them back for twoscore years or more. It was *Samoyede*, and very few dog lovers knew how to pronounce it. Just about the only ones who did were members of the well-heeled set, so the Sam became a canine status symbol for wealthy fanciers, and puppy prices stayed out of sight. Then in 1947, the name was shortened to *Samoyed*, a proper name that even bankrupt dog lovers could pronounce. Samoyed is pronounced Sam-a-yed—just the way Samoyede was pronounced, although people wouldn't believe it.

The Sam is one of the world's oldest purebreds and is also the senior sled dog. Today a majority of the best breeders are found in the midwestern and western states. There are very good pups elsewhere, but more caution is advised when buying.

Sams are probably not a good choice for anyone who worries about diet. The average Sam is unlike other breeds of her size, in that she is often a light or picky eater or just plain hard to please. Usually this is not cause for alarm, for a Sam seems to hold the proper weight by ignoring delicious, nutritious goodies. Owners of show dogs, of course, don't take chances and offer two or three little meals per day rather than one big one. There are some hearty eaters and gluttons in the clan, but a fat Sam is rare.

The dog is independent by nature, so training does require extra globs of patience. Otherwise, it's all clear sailing, providing the owner is not allergic to grooming. A good family dog, lovable and loyal, rarely a troublemaker and often the best friend of cats, the Sam can take any climate, and a city dog who looks like a gray Samoyed is really just in need of a dry cleaner.

The Sam's body is sturdy, strong, and a little long, but not so long that short legs impede the amazing driving power. The crowning glory is the double coat. The undercoat is soft, furry and dense, and at shedding time is avidly collected by nest-building songbirds. Some fanciers save it, card it, and knit it into warm socks, mittens and scarves. The topcoat is long, harsh and standoffish and forms a ruff around the neck and shoulders. The proper coat colors are solid white (by far the most popular), solid biscuit, white and biscuit, and cream.

Males stand 21 to 23½ inches and weigh fifty to fifty-five pounds. A good Sam's eyes are dark and almond shaped—blue eyes, even dark blues, disqualify for show.

## Siberian Husky (AKC, CKC)

Another gift from Siberia, Huskies were latecomers to the American world of dog shows, but that hasn't stopped them from becoming more popular and populous than the Sam. They also have more speed, are less difficult to groom, and have a name that everybody who speaks English can pronounce. Still, they did not come on strong as family pets until the early 1960s, when the breed started making an impression at dog shows. Long before then, however, the dogs had won fame as durable haulers of sleds for several famous explorers and as the stars of sled-dog races.

Huskies can be trained to do almost anything that is not beneath canine dignity, and they do almost as well in the city as in the country. The secret of success with this breed is to bring the pup home early (no later than the tenth week of age), lavish attention and affection, and start the training. This isn't always true with other breeds, but it is with the Huskies, and the earlier they get a fix on the people they will know, love and obey, the better for the dogs and the people. Still, even a properly bred, fed and trained Husky will disappear from view in a hurry if given a chance, for this breed dearly loves to run (for hours). If they are not supervised outdoors, an escape-proof yard or run, or personal supervision, is essential.

These are amiable, tractable dogs, but they're also loaded with energy and need more daily exercise than they can get walking on a leash. The double coat does not present any grooming problems, and the rumor that the ears are cropped is too ridiculous for further comment.

The body is close to short-coupled and the topcoat that blankets it is medium long, straight and fairly smooth-lying. Any coat colors are okay, solid or mixed; and matched head markings are usual.

A big male stands 23½ inches and weighs about sixty pounds. For show, the breed standard is very specific, and a dog taller than 23½ inches is disqualified. For a show bitch, 22 inches is maximum. Unlike the Sam, blue eyes are acceptable. So are brown eyes. So is one brown, one blue. So is a pair of blue-brown eyes. Whatever the colors, eyes must be almond shaped.

## Standard Schnauzer (AKC, CKC)

The Standard Schnauzer, developed in Germany a little over a century ago, and is the forefather of the Miniature Schnauzer, who is now much more abundant, proving nothing much. Cattle dogs at heart, Standard Schnauzers also asserted themselves as ratters, and that accidental talent won them AKC recognition in 1924 as terriers. It took twenty-one years to correct this harmless error. The CKC always knew that the Standard Schnauzer was a working dog, so reclassification was unnecessary in Canada.

These dogs haven't been used on cattle or vermin in a long time, but their high degree of canine intelligence hasn't been wasted, and in Europe they are honored for their work as army, police and guard dogs. Over here, their reputation is based on their performances as pet, show and Obedience dogs, and puppy quality is good. Since they're adaptable and don't care where they live—so long as they're living with the right people—Standard Schnauzers are good bets for the city. Even their coats don't seem to mind.

Although he might try to impress as the new tough guy in town, the Schnauzer is more bluff than fight, a little suspicious of strangers and a honey with people he knows. A spirited, fun-loving animal, this dog is very easy to train, would just as soon swim as trot, and doesn't ask for much beyond daily grooming. The grooming isn't much, but it's a little tricky at first. Check out the proper procedure with your pup's breeder at pickup time.

The short-coupled body is impressively strong and sturdy and wears a double coat. The tail is docked, and the ears are either cropped or uncropped. If cropped, they stand erect. The under-coat is always soft and well knit, and the topcoat is of medium length (1½ inches), harsh, wiry and thick. Luxuriant eyebrows, mustache and beard are common.

For show, eighteen to twenty inches is right for males, seventeen to nineteen inches for bitches. Being under or over those measurements means disqualification. A nineteen-incher carries about thirty-five pounds.

As for the Standard Schnauzer spinoff who's known as the Miniature Schnauzer, this smaller look-alike (10 inches is ideal for either sex) was developed by crossing undersized Standards with Affenpinschers (10½ inches, tops).

Bernese Mountain Dog, *above left,* courtesy of the owner, Mrs. Robert Redford. The actor's wife is a leading exponent of the breed in America. Siberian Husky, *above right,* owned by America's top breed authority, Mrs. Nicholas Demidoff, Monadnock Kennels. *(Bernice B. Perry)* Bearded Collies, below, courtesy of the owner, Mrs. Barbara Blake, Colbara Kennels, Canada. The adult is America's top winning show dog and the pup is seven weeks old. *(J. Guilfoyle)*

*Above,* Pulik in their corded coats, courtesy of the owners, Peg and Victor Stiff, Marvic Kennels. *(Curtis A. Reif) Below,* Rough Collies, all Obedience stars and owned by Susan Larson, Windhaven Kennels.

Standard Schnauzer,
courtesy of owner-breeders
Mary and Jerry Glazman,
Von Forhenhof Kennels.
*(Walter Whiteside)*

Bouviers des Flanders,
courtesy of Mrs. Ray
Hubbard, Madrone Ledge
Kennels. This dog is the
dam of the first bitch of the
breed to go Best in Show in
America. *(Brooks)*

Samoyed, *below*, courtesy of
Harold and Doris McLaughlin,
Silveracres Samoyed Kennel.
The eight-week-old pups on
the jacket are also from this
kennel.

# GROUP IV: TERRIERS
## Airedale Terrier (AKC, CKC)

You'd never guess from looking at them, but one of their ancestors is the Otter Hound. Some of the hunters thought they could improve on the Otter Hound and thus increase the otter harvest. The Airedale Terrier, the new breed, was dandy on otter and everything else, but, as reported earlier, England's otter population declined in a hurry—because of water pollution, not dogs. Since those sad otter days, or about 1880, the Airedale has developed into a general-purpose dog, and more so in America than elsewhere in the world. Depending on the whim of the owner, this terrier serves—often after very little training— as a hunting dog (for everything from rabbits to bears, upland birds and waterfowl), as a farm dog (herder, protector and destroyer of vermin), as a police dog and guide dog, as an Obedience and show star, and as a family pet. Old-timers who know older old-timers often refer to them as "ladies' guardians," and it is true that up until about 1919, many women wouldn't walk in public without an Airedale at their sides.

From 1900 to 1930, this was one of America's very popular breeds. The dangers involved in becoming even more popular were averted just in the nick of time by a sudden surge of interest in the Boxer, who became and still remains more popular. The Airedale went into a tailspin, and dropped thirty-odd places in the popularity rankings.

Happily, the only thing they lost was status. Airedales remain among the very best all-around dogs and are hard to beat in family circles. They're okay for city or country, are intensely loyal, and can be trained to accomplish any feat within the canine range.

Airedales are no longer ranked as the most popular of the terriers, but they remain the biggest of them all, and a scant fifty years ago they had more size than they have today. Up until the

1920s, they had more bone, broader heads, less length to the foreface, broader chests, far less tuckup and another inch or so of height. Overall, the refinements have probably been for the good, or at least they haven't hurt the breed. The contemporary Airedale Terrier has a clean-cut, trim look and the total effect is more pleasing to the eyes of dog fanciers, judges, breeders, and jet-set owners.

The body remains short-coupled and the coat is still a double. At a glance, Airedales don't seem to sport undercoats, but they do—very short and soft ones. The hard, wiry topcoat lies close and is colored in the traditional fashion: tan on head, ears, chest, belly, and most of legs (shoulders optional); black or dark grizzle on the sides and upper part of the body. White as a small blaze on the chest is considered legal, but anywhere on the rest of the dog is off limits.

A male stands about twenty-three inches and weighs close to fifty pounds. If you examine the breed standard, you won't read anything about a docked tail. Fortunately, you can read about it here. Yes, the Airedale wags a docked tail—about half the natural length and carried up.

## Bedlington Terrier (AKC, CKC)

Since 1937, the year the AKC granted this breed recognition, no all-breed dog show has been considered genuine until at least ten dog fanciers have proclaimed, "Look over there! Would you believe that sheep are being judged? That must be the puppy class in the ring. Puppies, lambs, get it? Ho, ho, ho!" That worn-out wit is probably as old as the breed, but it is useful for identifying brand-new dog fanciers at shows.

Yes, Bedlington Terriers look strikingly lamblike at first glance, but they've been around since about 1800 and are true terriers all the way. In their native England, they were developed to go after hare, badger and assorted vermin. In those days, the body was much longer, they ran around on shorter legs, the topline was level and the head was more Airedale type. But when dog shows came along, British breeders started refining Bedlingtons, and by 1875, they looked pretty much as they do today and were no longer working for a living. Strictly pet and show dogs.

Because of this breed's unusual appearance and gentle approach, dog lovers are apt to forget—if they ever knew—that Bedlingtons are tough cookies and able to take heat or cold in stride, as well as city or country living. They're lively, amazingly strong, anxious to learn and rarely forget what they've learned. Bedlingtons are a fine choice for the dog lover who is not awkward with comb and scissors, is willing to employ them daily, and can remember to brush out the coat every week. Left unattended, the coat tangles and knots in record time. The grooming isn't complex, but it should be regular.

The Bedlington Terrier lives in a farily compact body, but the roach back gives the illusion of length. The double coat is the usual soft and fine next to the skin, while the topcoat is hard, somewhat curly, and stands out from the body. For show, it's kept at about an inch. Owners of nonshow dogs usually keep the coats under two inches for easy grooming. Whatever the length, coats are colored blue, sandy and liver, or any one of those colors with tan—never solid white. It's as if Bedlingtons are willing to look something like lambs, but not entirely. They have canine dignity.

The ideal male stands 16½ inches and weighs about twenty pounds. Quality pups are the rule, and as adults, they come close to the ideal size or hit it right on the nose. In this one breed, pups of either sex are called yeanlings.

## Fox Terrier (AKC, CKC)

The claim that the Fox Terrier is the most popular purebred in the world is based on distribution, not numbers. One of the liveliest pooches in his size range, the Fox Terrier is found in all countries where canine ownership is legal. It would be hard to deny that the dog is the people's choice everywhere—among terrier lovers, at least.

The dog comes in two varieties, Smooth and Wire, and since 1930, the latter have outnumbered the former. However, it doesn't look like this will go on forever: in the last couple of years, more and more Smooths have been competing at shows, and it's dog fanciers who set the fashion for the general public in dogs.

Since both varieties are identical underneath their coats, the choice between them is slim. A few decades ago, breeding one variety to the other was common. While that's not supposed to happen today, it does, and it is only important if your choice is a Wire and you intend to show him. The dog's topcoat might not be hard enough to satisfy the judge.

This British breed was invented about two centuries ago for the purpose of "going to earth" (scrambling under ground level) after the likes of rats, foxes and badgers. In America, the Fox Terrier has served only as a pet, although most any representative of the breed finds it difficult to resist the challenge of a bold mouse, mole, chipmunk or toad.

Their world-wide distribution reflects their popularity as family pets who are a handy size for the smallest apartment and big enough for a castle in the wilderness. The chances of finding a quality Smooth pup involve less risk, based on the reality that pet shops usually offer only the Wires. Veteran Fox Terrier admirers who have lived under the same roof with both varieties vote for the Smooth as a better mixer, being less feisty and usually less noisy. The Smooth is also easier to groom, but that's not saying much, since a pet Wire requires only a mild brushing once or twice a week.

Under either coat, of course, the almost short-coupled body is identical, and that also goes for the docked tail. The Smooth coat is short, hard, dense and lies close. The Wire coat is also short, but harder and wiry. On both coats, white should predominate, with black and tan markings usual. For show, red, brindle and liver markings don't help.

The ideal male stands 15½ inches high and weighs about eighteen pounds. For show, either sex should be in hard condition, and that means more exercise than a Fox Terrier derives from jumping on and off furniture.

## Irish Terrier (AKC, CKC)

Ireland's liveliest contribution to the terrier clan is better known to American dog fanciers than to dog lovers, a sad state of affairs that should be corrected. If only a terrier will really satisfy, and you find the Airedale too big, the Fox too small and you just can't buy the looks of the Bedlington, then the Irish Terrier is one of the best choices around. Since pup demand has never been high, money breeders have overlooked this breed and quality is still on the high side.

Some people have the silly notion that coat care is too complex for them and that professional groomers charge too much for *stripping*. Don't let the word frighten you. A stripping comb ($2), fingers that don't shake and a little advice from a pup's breeder are all you need to *strip* (thin the coat) like an expert. This is done when needed, roughly two or three times a year, and the main idea is to keep the coat from becoming unkempt and shaggy. Or, if you have money to burn, the average professional charges $25 and up to strip (a dog).

Irish Terriers do well in the city (where a pro's fee for stripping is unrealistic), even if they were designed to go to earth and not through cement. They are willing, responsive and strong on remembering—three qualities that almost guarantee easy training. They're good travelers by car, full of fun on even the gloomiest day, and—like the Airedale—can be trained to satisfy the whim of the sportsminded. Add loyalty, durability and awareness of strangers to their string of virtues, and you have a dog that's just right for any terrier believer.

The body is a little long and looks streamlined, they show a little arch over the loins, a deep but not broad chest and a docked tail. A double coat, with the undercoat fine and soft and the topcoat dense, wiry and lying close. Coat color is either solid red (bright, golden, wheaten) or plain wheaten. Well, almost always, since a tiny patch of white on the chest, but not elsewhere, is okay for show.

A good size for a male is eighteen inches and about twenty-seven pounds. If the pup you buy has black hairs sprinkled among the red, don't panic. The unwanted black will disappear in the adult coat.

## Kerry Blue Terrier (AKC, CKC)

Another native of Ireland, the Kerry hails from County Kerry, reached America around 1900, waited until 1924 for the official AKC embrace, and is about at the Bedlington level in popularity. He no longer works at his original trades (anti-vermin, herding, guarding), and now serves as a family and show dog. The Kerry population would zoom if only more mothers knew that the coat is the next best thing to a 100 percent nonshedder, and the dog never leaves hair evidence of his recent presence on sofas, car seats and bedspreads.

Kerry quality in America is dandy. Pups rate from good to excellent, and about the only dim view to report on the breed is that grooming really should be daily. However, and happily, the task is not complex—it requires only a brush and comb—and it is a cinch compared to a Skye Terrier's coat, which is a shedder. The coat doesn't show city grime, the coat's wearer doesn't mind elevators or small apartments, and that combination qualifies the Kerry as a good bet for high-rise areas.

The average beast of the breed has a very agreeable temperament and is usually a good mixer with outsiders, human and canine. Training a Kerry isn't difficult, but a firm hand helps. In this breed, a pup's attention span is subnormal and the readiness for play is always strong. A Kerry often continues to act like a pup until the age of two or three years. If you like fun and games, buy a Kerry. If you are serious by nature, refrain.

This is a short-coupled, strong dog with smallish eyes and ears and a docked tail. The coat is soft, wavy and dense, and blue overall, with darker shadings okay in certain places. The blue runs from light blue-gray to deep slate, but is never the clear, bright blue of an unpolluted lake on a clear day.

A big male stands nineteen inches and weighs just under forty pounds. Pups are whelped as solid blacks; the blue starts showing at about six months, and the true coloration is usually established at eighteen months. A jet-black adult looks dramatic but can't be shown.

## Soft-Coated Wheaten Terrier (AKC)

These natives of Ireland have only been romping in the land of the free since 1948 and didn't become AKC card-holders until 1973. Since they've been chasing vermin and rounding up livestock on Irish farms for over 150 years, one wonders why it took so long for dog lovers to demand their appearance here. The Wheatens could be the oldest of Ireland's terriers and the ancestors of others, and they are among the few terriers who can be trained to perform like retrievers.

Like any other terriers, these dogs are activists at heart and really don't belong in a sedate environment. Otherwise, they have a couple of big virtues going for them that make them a great choice for a house or an apartment: they are not noisemakers and their coats qualify as nonshedders. You have to wonder why they aren't ten times as popular as they are. And until they become that popular, pup quality should stay as high as it is today.

Fun-loving, easy to train, amazingly quiet for a terrier, and bright as a button, the Wheaten is sure to please almost any anti-terrier person. The coat runs up to three inches and needs only a simple brushing a couple of times a week.

The Wheaten is a sturdy, deep-chested, close-coupled dog, and his tail is docked to two-thirds its natural length. The coat is soft, silky and a little wavy. Since the hairs are plentiful, the overall look is considered shaggy in some circles. Coat color is always an off-white, and the right tone is defined in several ways: pale gold, ripe wheat and light honey are closest.

A male Wheaten stands eighteen to nineteen inches and weighs up to forty-five pounds. Both male and bitch pups come into the world wearing reddish-brown coats, and it usually takes more than a year for the lighter, proper tone to take command. By the time coat color and texture are right—about twenty months— ears and muzzle may have become darker, and that's okay.

## Welsh Terrier (AKC, CKC)

Many people assume that the Welsh is a pocket edition of the Airedale. While they are look-alikes in some respects and were originally bred for the same duties, the two are separate breeds, and you can bet on that. The Welsh is much smaller, correspondingly lighter and a better fit in a crowded apartment. Two are better than one, of course, for the home that is peopleless during school and office hours. If bored, the nicest dog can create havoc.

Prior to 1960, impartial authorities agreed that the best dogs of the breed were found in England. Then a few Americans with good eyes for quality and a willingness to sign checks managed to buy and import some first-rate stock, and our breeders started closing the gap. Today the best Welsh dogs are found in America, although it is always wise not to brag about that when one is overseas.

These are lively, bouncing dogs, always ready for play and eager to please. As terriers go, they're average noisemakers, but count on them to bark up a storm when something doesn't seem right. For their size, they're pretty good watchdogs in the sense that their warning will awaken all deep sleepers within 150 yards.

*Above,* Smooth Fox Terrier, courtesy of Mrs. Fred Kuska, Crag Crest Kennels. This is an import from England.

*Right,* Wire Fox Terrier, courtesy of Mrs. Eve M. Ballich, owner-breeder, Evewire Kennels.

*Below,* Bedlington Terrier, courtesy of the R. Robert Helds, Adona Kennels.

*Above,* Airedale Terrier, courtesy of Mr. and Mrs. Albert Stevens, Pequod Kennels. *(William Gilbert)*

*Right,* Irish Terrier, courtesy of George Kidd for owner Martha Hall. *(Tauskey)*

*Below,* Welsh Terrier, ready and waiting for attention on grooming table, courtesy of Bardi McLennan, Bardwyn Kennels. Dog on jacket is courtesy of the Welsh Terrier Club of America.

Soft-coated Wheaten Terrier, courtesy of owners Emily W.
and Emily J. Holden. This dog, groomed for show, looks
less shaggy than normally. *(Ludwig)*

Kerry Blue Terrier, courtesy of owner Mrs. Brooke Postley,
Elbrley Kennels, who also owns the seven pups shown on
the jacket. *(John L. Ashbey)*

Welsh Terriers always look more serious than they really are, as if they were concerned about the brevity of their docked tails. They move their short-coupled bodies around on small, catlike feet, and wear coats that are hard, wiry and lie very close. Black and tan or black, grizzle and tan are the proper color combinations. Whatever the colors, a good coat is always quite dense and really should be stripped a couple of times a year (see discussion of Irish Terriers).

A male stands fifteen inches and weighs close to twenty pounds. Pups are mostly black when whelped, and the tan starts showing in the right places at from ten to twelve weeks.

# GROUP VI: NONSPORTING DOGS
## Chow Chow (AKC, CKC)

Chow Chows are smaller and more compact now than when they first came on the scene, and that—according to legend, art and scribbles—was two thousand years ago, give or take a couple of centuries. They were developed as hunting dogs in ancient China, but have always been regarded as pet and show dogs in the Western world. Until about fifty years ago, this unusual pooch was the favorite of high society. Then, as that society went down the drain, the Chow was discovered by true dog lovers.

Reliable breeders are found everywhere these days, and they still outnumber the kooks. Still, caution is advised. A bum Chow is hard to handle, but a good one is hard to beat as a canine pal. Even a good one isn't right for everybody, but she's just right for the dog lover who has a gentle hand, time for daily grooming and patience. You just can't rush this dog's training or always expect instant obedience. A Chow tends to make up her own mind about people, things and the time for action. She also travels in her own way: a stilted gait based on straight hind legs—so straight that they lack any angulation.

The Chow is noted for loyalty and affection toward those she knows, wouldn't consider taking a walk with a stranger and can be trusted to defend your home or apartment unto her last bark. Grooming is reasonably simple, amounting merely to brushing, and requires about five to ten minutes per day, depending upon the expertise of the brusher.

The dog's body is solid, squarish, and looks as immovable as a rock. The head is massive, the tongue is unique (blue-black) and the neck is that of a midget bull. The double coat is soft and woolly close to the skin, and the topcoat is thick, coarse, straight and standoffish. The ruff looks charged with electricity. Any solid color is okay, with lighter shadings on the ruff, breechings and tail. Red has always been the most popular coat color.

The average male stands twenty inches and weighs fifty pounds, but overall balance is considered more important than height and weight. Most red pups are born with black masks, but they fade away as the months go by.

## Dalmatian (AKC, CKC)

Spotted Dalmatians were trotting around Europe five hundred years ago and have been well known and dearly beloved in America since about 1890. They served people in many ways before achieving early fame in this country as coach dogs and the best canine friends a horse could have.

Any dog lover with normal vision recognizes the breed, but some admirers don't know that all Dal pups are whelped as solid white and wear pink noses. Within a day, the nose shows pigment, and at eight to ten days, faint smudges appear on the head and body. Those smudges get darker and more distinct as the weeks slip by, and almost all of the pup's permanent markings are in place by the twelfth week.

Some self-appointed "experts" insist that Dal pups are risky to buy because congenital deafness runs rampant in the breed. That's hogwash. An unscrupulous breeder might try to sell an occasional deaf pup, but only a moron would fail to recognize the defect. Pups don't develop deafness; they're deaf at birth in any breed.

These dogs are a good bet for city, country, mobile home and houseboat. They're friendly, easy to train, very clean in their habits, quiet most of the time, fun loving and never concerned about the weather. Happily, they seldom need any grooming. They need help with their nails, of course, and so does every other dog in the world. The same goes for exercise.

The Dalmatian body is a touch long, and both the tail and ears are natural. The coat is short, hard, dense and sleek as opposed to silky. These dogs are always white, with either black or liver markings, and the more distinct the spots are, the better for show. A white and black wears a black nose, but a white and liver should display a brown one.

An average male stands twenty-one inches and weighs a few pounds under fifty. For show, dogs over twenty-four inches are disqualified.

## Keeshond (AKC, CKC)

Imported from Holland in 1930, Keeshonds really deserve more popularity than they've achieved in America. The coat puts people off, since it looks like a problem to groom and keep in shape. Not so. A good weekly brushing is all that's needed for the coat worn by a pet Keeshond. The show coat, of course, should have daily attention.

Keeshond is pronounced Caze-hawnd, not Keys-haund, but these good-natured dogs don't care what you call them. Remarkably unchanged since about 1800, they originally served only as pets and later became popular as minor watchdogs on barges that crowded the waterways of both their native land and Germany. Today the sight of a barge doesn't excite them, and they are perfectly happy living with confirmed landlubbers.

The coat is the Keeshond's glory, and the dark markings around the eyes, called spectacles, set him apart from other breeds and help make him look as wise as an owl. The Keeshond is an alert pooch, above average in canine intelligence and a fast learner. Right at home in the city, where daily grooming is a must, the Keeshond is pretty much a one-family dog who likes to keep his people within view.

The Keeshond is a short-coupled, deep-chested dog who carries his natural tail in a tight curl over his rump. He wears a double coat, with the undercoat thick and downy and the topcoat a luxurious growth of long, standoffish hairs that are straight and harsh. The right color is wolfish, or a mix of gray and black, with black tips on the long hairs. For show, white markings are considered unbecoming.

A male Keeshond stands eighteen inches and weighs about thirty-five pounds. As for quality, most American breeding goes back to British imports, and the British Keeshond has long been rated superior to the Continental. These days, the breed is rated about equal in England and America, and some daring authorities (none British) suggest that our Keeshond is the best in all the world.

## Poodle (AKC, CKC)

The Poodle comes in three sizes or varieties, and our concern is with the biggest, the Standard Poodle, who happens to be the ancestor of the other two. In both the US and Canada, the Poodle has been ranked the most popular of the pure breeds since 1960, but whether the ranking is entirely fair depends upon how one feels about the fact that all three varieties are totaled as one. Rated on their own four feet, Standard Poodles would probably rank about thirtieth in popularity. The Miniature Poodle greatly outnumbers the Standard and is comfortably ahead of the Toy.

Although most people think that Poodles are natives of France, they really hail from fourteenth-century Germany. Developed as hunting dogs, or more specifically as retrievers, they were called many Teutonic names before *Pudel Hund* came along and stuck.

For a long time, they were among the best retrievers in the world and the great joy of sportsmen on both sides of the Atlantic. Standard Poodles didn't start to fade as hunting companions until about 1900, when their new and fancy show clips made them the darlings of society. Sadly, they are not used much in the field anymore, although small bands of hardy souls keep proving that Standards are still fine retrievers.

One look at a Standard Poodle show clip—English Saddle or Continental—is usually enough to discourage most dog lovers. Those clips do take up an enormous amount of grooming time, but there's no law that says a Poodle must wear either one for pet, Obedience, or field purposes. If you can handle a comb and scissors, just keep the coat full and at any desired length, and be proud of your dog's home-tailored kennel clip. A Standard Poodle tail without a pompom restores a touch of class to the breed.

Unless you have the misfortune to find a kooky breeder, your Standard Poodle pup will develop an amazing quota of canine intelligence. This breed is one of the brightest around, and your dog can be taught to do almost anything short of reading, writing and cooking. Although they are very popular in the city, that's not the place for them. The smaller editions are better suited to metropolitan living.

The body is squarish and almost short-coupled, and the high-set tail is docked. The coat is dense and harsh to the touch, and any solid color is okay. For show, shadings of the same color are permitted. In any color, the coat qualifies as an almost nonshedder.

Any Poodle standing over fifteen inches is a Standard, and one who stands twenty inches will weigh close to forty-five pounds. For the record, a Toy stands up to ten inches, and a Miniature is always over ten inches but never more than fifteen.

## Tibetan Terrier (AKC, CKC)

Members in good standing at the AKC since 1973, Tibetan

Terriers are really from Tibet, but they're not really terriers and nobody cares. They're also not a pint-sized version of the Old English Sheepdog, even if a fully grown Tibetan does resemble an Old English pup. For easy identification, look to the tails: Tibetans carry theirs up and over the back.

Almost all that is known about Tibetan Terrier history is based on rumors, and of those, the most interesting concern the celebrated holy men of Tibet. Supposedly, the monks were the principal breeders of these pooches, and often gave surplus pups as gifts to weary travelers of distinction. This went on for centuries, but the dogs remained unknown to the outside world until the early 1920s. How the Tibetan Terrier got out of Tibet also remains in the rumor stage and is not very interesting.

Tibetans are smart, active dogs, always ready for fun, intensely loyal, and quiet for their size. Among the most agreeable of the shaggy dogs, they will try just about anything, including herding and flushing upland birds. The simple grooming is a weekly affair.

This non-terrier's body is quite compact and surprisingly powerful. A double coat hides the boxlike conformation, and it's the usual soft and dense next to the skin. The topcoat is long, fine and fairly straight, and the right colors are white, cream, gray, black, golden and smoke. The coat can be one color or a mix of two or three. The lighter the coat, of course, the less suitable for the city.

A big Tibetan Terrier will stand sixteen inches and weigh twenty-five to thirty pounds. In case you're wondering, the other Tibetan breeds currently in America are the Lhasa Apso, the Tibetan Spaniel and the Tibetan Mastiff. China gets credit for the little Shih Tzu, but sixty years ago that dog was known to Americans as the Tibetan Poodle. No wonder Toy Poodles are confused.

*Above,* Chow Chow, courtesy
of the owner, Frances I. Reid,
K'wan Rei House of Chows.
*(Olan Mills)*

*Right,* Dalamatian, courtesy
of owner-breeder Amy
Lipschutz, Dottidale Kennels.
*(Tauskey)*

*Below,* Keeshond, courtesy
of Mr. and Mrs. Edwin
Cummings, Wynfomeer
Kennels. *(Tauskey)*

Standard Poodle completing an Open exercise in Obedience. High jump is set at 1½ times the dog's height. Courtesy of Kae Reiley, Kaeley Kennels. *(Tom O'Shea, Gaines)* The poodle on jacket is shown at age fifteen and is owned by Miss Christa Skeibe.

Tibetan Terrier, courtesy of the owners, Jane and George Reif, Shaggar Kennels. *(Curtis A. Reif)*

## PRESENT, PURE AND STILL UNRECOGNIZED

## Greater Swiss Mountain Dog

Another member of the Swiss *Sennenhunde* family, and a more recent arrival (1968) than his cousin the Bernese Mountain Dog, the Greater Swiss has been attracting recognized reliable breeders to the fold, and the breed future looks dandy. Five years ago the wait for a quality pup often took up to a year. Today the quality is just as high and the wait is short, often no longer than it takes to place a telephone call. The big beast is now found in seventeen states.

If you liked the looks of the Bernese but thought you'd prefer a bigger dog, then the Greater Swiss is just what your banker ordered. He can haul heavier loads, pull more small fry in a pony cart and make more of a splash in the swimming pool. Otherwise, his looks and virtues closely resemble those of the Bernese, although his double coat is a little shorter. A less likely bet for the city.

An ideal male stands twenty-eight inches and weighs 130 pounds. Although he is not naturally aggressive, the size makes strangers wary, and the end result makes him an ideal, if accidental watchdog.

## Portuguese Water Dog

Of all the dogs who don't mind getting their feet wet, Portuguese Water Dogs rate with the best as swimmers and have no equals as deep divers and underwater paddlers. These dogs are untold centuries old, but old enough to be considered the probable ancestors of both Irish Water Spaniels and Poodles.

The Portuguese Water Dog gained fame as the fisherman's friend in the days of the big fishing fleets. He was used to carry messages from ship to ship and to shore, to retrieve tackle and gear that had fallen overboard, to recover fish that had jumped the nets and to guard the rum kegs for the first mate. The Water Dogs who stayed home and on dry land often herded goats and sheep, and sometimes fetched game and fowl for lucky hunters. On land and sea, the dog has always been regarded as a fine companion and pet.

This remarkable canine was close to extinction two decades ago, but a few alarmed American dog lovers got into the act, and today this country is home to more Portuguese Water Dog breeders than any other country in the world, not excluding Portugal. It follows that there are more dogs of this breed in America than anywhere else, but what's even more important is that the quality remains consistent. There are none better anywhere.

While the American-bred Portuguese Water Dog takes to water like a duck, he can get along without swimming and diving, adjusts to city life and dotes on people. The dog gets along socially with other pooches, is reasonably easy to train, is known for his even temperament, and usually worries when a person he loves is swimming. And like his descendant, the Irish Water Spaniel, the Portuguese Water Dog is a clown at heart and can lift your spirits on a gloomy day.

This short-coupled dog comes with natural ears and tail, wears either a wavy or curly coat, and in one or the other, looks a little shaggy. Solid blacks or browns are usual, and touches of white are permissible. Black or brown, the coat is a nonshedder.

A big male will stand twenty-two inches and weigh fifty-five pounds, while a small bitch will stand sixteen inches and go thirty-five pounds. There's still quite a spread in size, but nobody really minds, and people who are allergic to dog hairs mind least of all. Almost always, a person who can't look at a dog without weeping or sneezing finds that he or she can live in healthy harmony with this breed.

*     *     *

# PRESENT, UNPURE AND POPULAR
## Americanis

The ancestry of this dog is different from that of any other breed found in this book or in the world. In tracing the origins of breeds, the family trees of a minority are pretty well known, while those of the majority will always remain mysteries. As for the latter, breed historians report the lack of information in different ways, such as referring to origins as "clouded in the mists of antiquity" and "probable, but not reported in any manuscript" or "lost in the halls of time immemorial."

Well now, the origins of the Americanis are just as lost to us as those of many breeds, but the dog is different because the very recent origins are rarely a matter of record. You might say that this breed is still evolving and that it will never be standardized in the sense of there being a known number of varieties. The Americanis has always been, and always will be, an unfinished breed.

Despite the fact that all purebreds (and their owners) tend to rate the Americanis as socially inferior, dogs of this family outnumber the grand total of purebreds found in any other fifty breeds you care to name. If popularity is based on numbers, then the Americanis is the number-one pooch in America, no matter how you feel about the Poodle.

Admittedly, the Americanis also has more critics than any other fifty breeds, and most of the time, the critics are either dog fanciers or people who have never owned a dog. But although nobody on earth can predict the future size, temperament and personality of an Americanis pup, every year tens of thousands of dogs who belong to this unfinished breed are making their owners very happy. While none are born as specialists, many can be trained to perform desired chores, and you must know, if you keep up with the news, that these dogs perform heroic deeds as often as purebreds.

*Above,* Greater Swiss Mountain Dog, the biggest new breed on the American scene. Courtesy of the owner, Barry Luther. (*J. Jackson*) Pup on the jacket is owned by Mrs. J. F. Hoffman, Carinthia Kennels.

*Left,* Americanis in the White House. Miss Amy named him Grits. (*UPI*)

*Below,* Portuguese Water Dog, courtesy of the owner, Mrs. Jon R. Schneller. This dog is only ten months old.

These dogs cannot, of course, compete in the dog game's formal sports, and in view of the canine surplus, it doesn't make sense to use them for breeding. If those facts don't matter and you decide that an Americanis is the only dog for you, it may take a little time to find the right pup. When you do, check him or her out with your vet before making a final decision. If you're right for each other, the pup will return your love tenfold.

## IN REFERENCE TO ANY BREED

When it comes to personal hygiene, pet dogs can't do everything for themselves, and they can't stay in the pink of condition without help from their owners. Just another way in which you must go more than halfway with your dog, whatever the breed. The name of the game is grooming, and it is played in three parts:

1. Coat. Single coats require the least care. Depending upon length, application of comb or brush or both, weekly or twice weekly is sufficient. The idea is to remove dead and dying hairs and make room for new growth, and the removals become more frequent when the dog is actually shedding. The double coat is a little more trouble, since hairs in both undercoat and topcoat are dying on a continual basis, and dying at a wholesale rate during the customary spring and fall sheddings.

The tools of the trade are a comb, a brush and sometimes a curry. Rely on the breeder's advice, buy only the tools you need and avoid the many impractical, expensive offerings. Two or three dollars each will buy the best of these grooming aides.

2. Nails. For pup or adult of either sex, canine toenails keep growing, but millions of owners pay no attention. Thus, more millions of dogs walk around all their lives on poor and sometimes painful feet. Nails are at their proper length when you can't hear them click as the dog walks or trots across a wooden or linoleum floor. In other words, keep them just short of the ground.

It's easy to keep them short with a manual pet nail clipper, and a good one costs about three dollars. Or you can spend ten times as much for an electric nail trimmer (really a file) that grinds away excess nail. With either one, stop at least a quarter-inch before the *quick*, or a half-inch if you are the nervous type. The quick is the blood vessel that runs half-way down the nail. Check a pup's nails at least every two weeks, an adult's every three.

3. Ears. The longer the dog's ears, the greater the likelihood of trouble, and long droopers are the ones to really watch. Most of the time, a dog with ear problems gives off a musty, unpleasant odor.

Moist ears, the beginning of trouble, are caused by poor air circulation. Douse the inner ear with antiseptic powder and thin out the excessive hair and any sticky exudate with your fingers (thumb and index). Don't use scissors, tweezers, razor blades or any other tools, and stay very clear of the ear canal. If additional cleaning is warranted, use a mixture of water and peroxide in a ratio of 20 to 1 and apply gently with cotton swab sticks. Use a little more powder to help the ear dry. The goal is a dry, clean ear with free air circulation.

If you have money to burn, your friendly veterinarian will take care of your dog's nails and ears. Of course, if you're that helpless, maybe you don't deserve a dog. Loyalty is a two-way street.

# 4

# The Search for the Right Pup

Over four million purebred pups will be sold in America this year, and nobody in the dog game will be surprised if the total reaches five million. The puppy saturation point has not been reached and may never be reached. Since World War II, purebred puppies have become very big business.

## Breeders

The people responsible for producing pups are all classified as breeders. About 75 percent of the active ones are *hobby breeders*, and most are overjoyed to break even from the sale of their pups. The best of the breeders turn out America's quality pups, and the others rate bows for pups that range from fairly good to quite average. If they've been around long enough, many can point with pride to several first-rate dogs. Almost always, the worst hobby breeder in town is a less risky source than the nearest *commercial breeder*, who breeds dogs for a living either full- or part-time.

Since the hobby breeding of purebreds came into vogue, women have always outnumbered men, and married women are more numerous in the field than the singles. Once in a while, a husband tires of seeing his wife work so hard for so little, and convinces her that money can be made in raising dogs. To do this requires more time and work than one person can handle, so they join hands and become commercial breeders.

There are three hobby breeders for every commercial breeder, but the latter produce about half the purebred pups that exchange hands for money each year. The biggest of these operators are known as puppy farmers, and they are the major puppy suppliers for pet stores, department stores, mail-order houses, prize contests, animal auctions and bargain-basement sales. In a merchandising sense, the puppy farmers are both manufacturers and wholesalers, and what they produce is never worth the eventual retail price, or even the original low-low wholesale price.

While puppy farmers are found in most states and Canada, Kansas is still home to the most and the biggest, with Missouri and Iowa running close. These three states provide better than 40 percent of the country's mass-produced pups. The pups are shipped to distant markets, but that doesn't mean that pet stores in the midwest offer pups of quality. Southern puppy farmers ship their living wares to the midwest.

Wherever they are whelped and however they are priced, these mass-produced pups are bummers. Naive dog lovers buy them for one reason or another, quite often on impulse and without much thought. Yes, the cute pet-shop pup is a purebred, with the papers to prove it, but those legitimate papers reveal absolutely nothing about the pup's sire and dam—beyond the fact that they are also purebreds. There's no way of knowing what defects the pup may have inherited, and it's a cinch that the little charmer was weaned too early, shipped too soon, fed a variety of wrong diets and put through a series of traumatic experiences that won't help his future.

Puppy farmers are big-time commercial breeders. All deal in more than one breed, and the same is often true of those who run smaller operations and produce only a few hundred, rather than thousands of pups per year. Some of the lesser producers are former hobby breeders who still claim that status, and most are easily recognized by their related canine businesses of boarding, grooming, selling dog furnishings and equipment or actually running a pet store.

The search for the right puppy really begins with the search for the right breeder. If you find a commercial breeder at the end of your rainbow, you are a hopeless gambler and should reform before following a new trail. You'll save yourself time, money, and heartache if you confine your hunt to hobby breeders who live within convenient visiting range. These breeders come from every walk of life, their experience counts more than their social status, the best are seldom the biggest, and each can be rated as one of the following:

**Outbreeder:** one who mates unrelated dogs of the same breed. Most breeders—perhaps as many as 90 percent—are in this category, and many of them don't know it. Although one can be very serious about outbreeding, there's nothing very scientific about it, and luck plays as important a role as the involved genes. The breeder hopes that the pups will retain the good points of both parents and not reflect any of their faults. This sometimes happens, but rarely to an entire litter. A good pup or two per litter is more likely, but even that doesn't happen consistently.

What does happen consistently is that the majority of the dogs judged to be the best purebreds in America are the results of outbreeding. This fact probably contributes to the great popularity of outbreeding, although the law of averages accounts for their successes—with so many millions of outbreds running around, a few thousand ought to be good.

On the positive side, it can be said that any outbred pup is a much better bet than the average inbred pup.

**Inbreeder:** one who mates closely related dogs. Closely related dogs belong to an immediate family: father and son, mother and daughter. These four provide three opportunities for inbreeding:

father to daughter, mother to son, and brother to sister. Any of those matings intensifies the known dominant genes and stamps the entire litter with desired virtues, while hopefully eliminating or reducing unwanted faults.

This breeding method is practiced by hobbyists who seek perfection in a hurry and hope to achieve it by taking the laws of nature into their own hands. This works out on paper, but rarely in real life and infrequently beyond the second generation. While the mating of known, positive genes (representing desired virtues) should and often does result in beautiful pups, inbreeding also magnifies the recessive genes (undesirable faults) carried by sire or dam. Although neither of the parents is afflicted, either or both can be carriers of the unwanted recessives which they pass on to their pups. And as these beautiful pups mature, they start showing the sins of their forebears. These may include the wrong bite or tail or eye colors for their breed, or something as unfortunate as hip dysplasia or as tragic as an eye disease that leads to blindness.

That's not the only danger of inbreeding: while it is possible to retain good temperament for one generation, it is seemingly impossible to extend it into the second. So any inbred pup is a gamble, even if the breeder is the wife of the mayor, or your school's principal, or a movie star. Fortunately for both the canine world and the general public, inbreeding is practiced only by a few—less than one percent of all hobby breeders.

**Linebreeder:** one who mates related dogs of a family strain who are not of the same or the succeeding generation. Linebreeding, considered a compromise of the other two methods, is a sensible improvement on inbreeding. Matings are never closer than generations one and three (grandfather to granddaughter), and both dogs are selected for their superior conformations and desired temperaments. This is what the science of breeding is all about, and what the thinking breeders of dogs, cattle and horses have been practicing for over a century.

Pups from a linebred litter represent the best quality, granted that the breeder is not kennel blind or faulty in some other respect. On a percentage basis, a linebred pup is a much better bet than an outbred one and a far better bet than an inbred. However, finding a linebreeder can take a little extra time. They represent the minority among hobby breeders, or about ten percent. Most are veterans in the dog game.

Inbreeders know who they are and make no bones about it. The same goes for linebreeders, but puppy buyers looking for such a hobbyist can sometimes be misled by outbreeders who think of themselves as linebreeders. A pup's pedigree tells the story. Just study the names of the parents, grandparents, and great-grandparents, properly known as sires and dams, grandsires and granddams, and great-grandsires and great-granddams. If several of the names in the sire's family tree correspond to those in the dam's, chances are that the pup is indeed linebred. When in doubt, double check with the breeder.

No matter the method, any hobby breeder proudly refers to his or her *kennel*, and sometimes that kennel is difficult to see. The kennel need not be a building with attached runs. Many of the best breeders confine their operations to the home, and pups are whelped and kept in a corner of the kitchen where someone can keep an eye on them. While all quality pups aren't found in small- and medium-size kennels, the chances for good pups decrease as the kennel size increases. For those who wonder about size, a kennel with more than five active brood bitches is big, one with ten is too big; and one with twenty is ridiculous. The canine thrives on human association, and the hobby breeder who spreads herself or himself too thin isn't too bright. Socially speaking, the pups get a bum start in life.

If all of the above about breeders and kennels strikes you as unimportant, so be it. You could be right, but only if you're also outrageously lucky. The happiest one-dog owners I know are the ones who spent plenty of looking-around time before spending their money. Usually the time consumed can be credited to caution. In the dog game, caution is summed up in two words: *buy slowly*. Once you've found the right breeder and he or she has shown you the right pup, buy slowly—satisfy yourself on these points:

**Puppy Health.** The pup should be lean and lively, not thin or fat. Eyes should be clear, nose moist but not runny, ears clean (insides pink), teeth white and gums pink and firm.

Forget the pup who snorts or sneezes, whose coat is smelly or dirty, or whose littermates are sluggish or do not pass the health test noted above. This will not be the right breeder, after all.

**Puppy Temperament.** The pup should be lively, and that means outgoing, friendly and playful. Sometimes one pup is an obvious bully, which is an early sign of stubbornness. An extrapatient owner will be needed.

Forget the shy pup, as noted previously. If you notice two shy pups, consider forgetting the entire litter, since the inherited factor may be present and not yet showing in all the other pups. If the dam of the litter seems shy, run for the nearest exit.

**Environment As You Find It.** If there's a strong canine scent in the air or the puppy run isn't clean, you've come to the wrong kennel. When pups under ten weeks old aren't sleeping and playing, they're eating and drinking and—as the saying goes—relieving themselves. The result is messy, the mess is repeated numerous times per day, and the responsibility for cleanups, scrubbings and disinfectings belongs to the breeder. Unattractive aroma and visible filth are signs of a careless breeder, and the pups will be purebred troubles. Promise to come back in a few days—and break the promise.

**Puppy's Family Tree.** Whether the pup is purebred or not, any pup has a pedigree. A dog's family tree amounts to the names of the dogs who are his or her true ancestors, the ones in both sexes who preceded this dog on this earth. Thanks to inherited genes, some dominant and some recessive (and each can be desirable or not, from the human viewpoint), a pup is the sum total of all her or his ancestors, in both body and character.

Those with the most influence, of course, are the dam and sire. When you visit a litter of pups at a hobby breeder's kennel, you'll always have a chance to meet the dam. After all she's been through, she won't be in top physical shape, but if she seems nasty or bites you, don't trust any of her pups. As for the dam's parents, and the sire and his parents, and any other dogs in the family tree, the more you are able to meet, the broader and wiser your look into a pup's future. Any hobby breeder who has been in the dog game for ten years or so will have a few of the pup's ancestors on the premises. If you don't like what you see, don't buy.

There are a couple of important things to remember about inheritance: (1) It dilutes rapidly from generation to generation, and influence is based on relative closeness. Thus, if Mom looks strange for her breed, Junior's chances of becoming as handsome as his grandsire, a famous show champion, aren't much. (2) An acquired characteristic cannot be inherited. Accordingly, a Beagle trained to climb ladders cannot pass along this talent to his sons and daughters, and the untrained Airedale who points game birds like a Pointer does not hand on this unusual breed accomplishment.

## Understanding Hobby Breeders

Much as they might like to, most hobby breeders just don't have the room to keep all or most of the pups in every litter. If they practice linebreeding, they'll keep one or two, but otherwise selling the pups is usual—if only to raise funds to cover the red ink and start planning next year's litter with a clear conscience.

Because more and more people have been buying purebreds

over the last few decades, most breeders know that they'll sell their pups. Sometimes, of course, too many litters of the same breed are available in one area. When that happens, the selling of pups gets competitive, but not in the pricing.

Breeders usually hold to their asking price through thick and thin. After all the trouble they've been through—the proper raising of pups is not a picnic—they really can't be blamed for expecting true value for their little bundles of joy. In the great majority of the pure breeds, no matter where you reside, the average price tag for a quality male pup ranges from $100 to $150, and that's just about what it was fifty years ago. Can you think of anything else that hasn't doubled in price in that time span?

It must be admitted that many over-anxious breeders try every trick in the book to sell their pups as soon as possible. Any breeder who moves out baby canines before they're old enough should be avoided as surely as the sinners with dirty, unkempt kennels. Eight weeks of age is about the right time to sell pups in most breeds, although a few days earlier or a few weeks more won't matter.

Hard-sell artists are probably more numerous than card sharks. They come in many guises, but all consider the sale of each pup as an urgent matter and leave no promotional stone unturned to make that sale. If the hard-sell breeder has a motto, it's probably "Promise him anything, but sell him a puppy."

How does one know when a hobby breeder is gold rather than glitter? When the breeder is more interested in you than in selling you a pup. If that answer seems too simple or foolish, consider this:

A responsible breeder has more than the future of the breed invested in the pups. It's taken huge amounts of planning, selecting, time, labor, expense and devotion to bring those pups into the world and to a saleable age, and the breeder is not about to sell a single one to just any dog lover who comes along. So be pleased if he or she seems to ask more questions about you than you do about the pups. The breeder wants to be sure that you're the right dog lover: a person who can provide the proper environment and who has the time for care and training and companionship.

## Hip Dysplasia

Since you'll be asked some personal questions, it will be fair for you to ask questions in return. If the breed runs to weights over forty pounds, be sure to ask, "What about OFA certifications?"

The OFA is the Orthopedic Foundation for Animals and is regarded as the clearinghouse for conscientious breeders who want to make sure that their dogs are okay in the hip department. The issue is *hip dysplasia* (HD), a physical defect that is known to occur in all breeds, although it is quite rare in the Whippet and Greyhound. Just as shyness is considered a major personality sin, HD is regarded as the biggest physical sin, and usually it is inherited. Although it has been the subject of intensive research over the past forty years, the average dog lover hasn't heard about HD or thinks his dog is suffering from arthritis. New breeders are sometimes unaware of it, and many breeders refuse to talk about it and hope it will go away. That's unlikely, and you can bet your hat that the breeder who will discuss HD without flinching takes canine health seriously.

If HD is news to you, it amounts to an improper fit of the femur head (the bone at the top of the hind leg) and the hip joint. Cases can be so mild that they aren't apparent to the eye or so severe that the dog is crippled and in pain when he or she moves. Mild or severe, it would be great for dogdom if all breeders would refrain from mating HD dogs, but that's not the case. To date, hobby breeders of giant dogs and sporting dogs have been the most concerned. The most reliable of these breeders will be happy (and proud) to show a Dysplasia Control Registry certificate from the OFA for both the sire and the dam of the litter. The certificate means that OFA experts have studied radiographs of the dogs, found no evidence of HD, and okayed both for breeding. Their pups stand the best change of not developing HD, although there's no such thing as a guarantee against it; it has been known to skip generations.

One of the strange things about canine HD is that every pup is apparently born without it and remains free of it through the earliest months. That's true no matter the condition of hips of both parents. Then, somewhere along the line, the pup destined by inheritance to carry HD starts developing it. Bad hips seldom pop up before five months of age, and detection that early is done by X ray. Usually, the pup who achieves adulthood with clean hips will remain sound, and almost always the dog who is sound at twenty-four months is home free and safe for breeding. The OFA does not clear dogs under that age.

All the above concerns *inherited HD*, and it seems to apply in the majority of known cases. There is another type that for our purposes will be known as *stupid HD*. The reference is to those puppy owners who insist that baby canines aren't healthy unless they are kept in a fat and round condition. These silly overfeeders, often puffy and jolly themselves, defy both the laws of nature and the facts of life. Any puppy—purebred or Americanis—comes into the world with extremely soft bones, very fluid joints and an enormous appetite. In all but the tiny toy breeds, the bones stay quite soft during the first ten months, and overweight will cause excessive strain on the hind legs and hip sockets. When the vet finds the pup has HD, the owner blames the breeder. Sometimes the sincerest hobby breeders can't win.

So much for the short course on HD. There is no cure, but some cases can be relieved by surgery, and the operation is costly. In a severe case, the afflicted dog may or may not emit sounds of pain, but his hind legs will drag as he trots along, he will have trouble getting to his feet and usually he's lame. If your favorite breed runs forty pounds or more, you will be foolish if you buy a pup whose sire and dam do not have OFA clearance. And if the breed runs over seventy-five pounds (the giants), you are a complete idiot if you buy such a pup.

\*          \*          \*

## The Purebred's Papers

Every purebred pup has, or should have, papers to prove his or her age, breed, sex, parentage, ownership and less important matters. Although commonly referred to in the plural, the papers are actually a single piece of paper that makes the pup official and socially acceptable at the American Kennel Club. It is the formal breed-registration application for the individual pup, and when properly signed, it is also a transfer of ownership from breeder to new owner.

When you buy a purebred pup, you are entitled to this paper, and the breeder should sign it as you are handing over the payment for the pup. To safeguard against loss by accident or misplacement, it's wise to complete this application before the new moon. Sign it in the right places, jot down your first and second choices for the pup's name, put the completed form and $4 into an envelope and mail same to the AKC. If all is in order, the AKC will return the pup's individual registration form to you. This will carry the pup's official name and number.

There are a few things to watch out for when you are inventing first and second choices of names for a pup. A name can consist of several words, such as Dreamboat Dan of Windy Hill, but it cannot employ more than twenty-five letters, as in Dreamboat Daniel of Windy Hill. And although a few slip through every year, the pup should not be named after a person, especially a celebrity. The idea behind making two choices, of course, is to avoid duplication of another, already-registered dog's name.

Most purebreds remain unaware of their often cumbersome official names, and that's why Seashore Sweetsue comes on the run when she hears her master call for Annie.

## More Paperwork

Although they are not required to do so by law or the AKC, considerate breeders supply additional papers to puppy buyers. The breeder who doesn't really should, and if he or she doesn't upon request, put your money back in your pocket. First, evidence of health:

1. Proof of temporary shot. Usually a certificate from the breeder's vet showing date and type of inoculation. Your vet will want to see this in order to determine the timing of future, permanent shots.

2. Proof of first worming. Same as above. Play it safe and don't buy an unwormed pup.

If you study the classified ads in local papers, you'll note that more and more breeders are offering pups with "health guaranteed." In most cases, this means that you can return the pup within a specified number of days if your vet finds that the pup is not healthy. If the guarantee is for money back, it's an honest deal, but if it means exchange for another puppy, it's a gimmick to be avoided.

Onward to genealogy:

3. The pup's pedigree. You are entitled to a gratis copy of this, and the breeder who charges or refuses to supply one should be run out of town. Any ethical breeder will gladly hand over a three-generation pedigree, going all the way back to the pup's sixteen grandparents, and given a little time, most breeders will prepare a five-generation one. Your pup's pedigree won't mean a thing to the dog, but it gives you bragging rights, dinner conversation and something to frame. It also saves research time in the event that you decide to become a hobby breeder.

The only other paper that you might be interested in is really a contract, and it's known as BT, which is short for breeder's terms. This is a solution for many purebred puppy buyers who are enduring a shortage of cash, but it's something that you can't very well look for. Almost always, BT finds you, and usually it comes about when a hobby breeder learns of your yen for a good pup, discovers that you can't afford the asking price, and likes your looks and home situation. The breeder offers you a pup for free or at a ridiculously low price, but either way there are certain conditions, or terms. BT is a fairly common practice with linebreeders who don't have room for more than three or four adult dogs and need twice as many to keep their breeding programs rolling along. Since they can't hang onto their very best pups, they farm them out on BT to dog lovers who want the best but lack the funds.

Here's how BT often works in the case of a male pup. You become the owner, but the breeder may use him (when he's old enough) at stud for a specified number of times with no fee. In the case of a bitch pup, you would promise to eventually breed her at least once to a stud dog of the breeder's choice, then raise the litter to eight weeks and give a prearranged number of pups to the breeder.

BT can be the thrifty way to ownership of a very good purebred. Of course, your parents would have to agree, and one of them would have to sign on the dotted line as your legal representative.

## Acquiring an Americanis

Since hobby breeders do not deal in the non-AKC Americanis, pooches of that canine family do not come with papers of any kind. It is never difficult to find an Americanis pup, for the supply always exceeds the demand in every season, and prices range from zero to a few dollars. There are no two ways about it—you'll save a bundle if you start with an Americanis, but supporting one in the manner expected by any pet dog will cost as much as supporting a purebred of the same size.

Americanis breeders usually earn that distinction through carelessness, in that they failed to note that their pet bitches were in season or did note it and failed to confine their beloveds, or never did understand the sex life of canines. Whatever the reason, they are usually accidental breeders and are most anxious to unload the pups before the little guests become an unwanted expense. So the pups very often go to their new homes after they've been weaned but before they're ready: too young, unwormed, and not inoculated. Unless you happen to know that the breeder has taken proper care of the pups, and you like their dam, then you are no better off than the gambler who pays big money for a pup at a pet store.

The best place to find a healthy Americanis pup is at a nonprofit animal shelter run by a humane society or an animal welfare league. On any day of the week, any shelter has a variety of pups on hand, and it's difficult not to find several in the desired sex, coat and color. Finding a pup who will please is seldom a problem, but convincing management that you're the right person for the pup can be one. The shelter is in the business of finding good homes for its pups and other pets. If you live in a palace and are the irresponsible offspring of parents who think dogs should run free at all times, yours is not a good home.

A shelter's size and operating budget determine the number of dogs on hand and the conditions for transfer of ownership. The best evidence that the shelters are sincere about finding good homes is the fact that they place an average of only ten percent of their dogs each year, most of them pups. After a reasonable holding period, dogs that remain unplaced must be destroyed to make room for new arrivals. Unfortunate, yes, but that's the way it is.

Release rules vary from shelter to shelter, but at an average one all pups are wormed, up to date on inoculations, and in the pink of condition. Bitch pups may or may not be spayed. If she is not, the new owner must agree to have the pup spayed within a specified time period. Sometimes the shelter can arrange for low-cost or no-cost surgery. The neutering of a male pup may also be part of the release terms.

And finally, sometimes there's a modest fee that the shelter prefers to call a contribution. In a very small way, this helps the shelter pay its considerable bills. Figure on a high of $20—much less than it cost the shelter to keep the pup in condition and ready for a new home.

Purebreds are also available at animal shelters, although on a sometimes basis, and the release rules are the same for them. You have to be born lucky to find the breed you're looking for, and it helps to visit the right shelter at the right time. When they are available, purebred pups rarely come equipped with papers of any kind, and the chances of registering them with the AKC are small. There's always a chance of getting a listed number, however, and this means that the pup has at least one privilege more than an Americanis: the right to compete in the sport of Obedience.

Usually, the purebreds you find at shelters are adults, and occasionally those adults do have formal papers. For both those adult purebreds who do and those who don't, and all adult Americanis as well, let it be known that they will often satisfy as much as, and even more than, pups. While first-time dog owners rush to pups the way thirsty camels run to water, there's something to be said about bringing home an older dog. You know what you're getting in terms of coat, color, general appearance and size. You should also be able to judge the dog's temperament. It's set and it won't change much no matter what you do. If your source is a shelter, then you can be sure the dog is in good health and not about to cost you a fortune in vet's bills.

Indeed, the only major risk concerns the dog's idiosyncrasies, if any. Does he chase cats in the afternoon, or prefer rag rugs to hamburg, or howl when he watches television, or claim the sofa as his own, or obey commands only when he feels like it—and that's not too often? Fortunately, it's often possible to eliminate that risk by talking to the former owner, the person who placed the dog in the shelter for some legitimate reason, such as moving, a death in the family or a new wife who is allergic to dog hairs.

You are not as bright as your school grades indicate if you acquire an adult on faith alone. Do your best to uncover the bad news, if any, and decide whether you can tolerate it. The full-grown pooch will respond to your care and learn to love you, but canine love does not include self-improvement. You must learn to live with the dog you choose pretty much as is. If you can't do that, go for a pup.

# 5

# The New Pup in Your Life

A healthy pup spends the first seven weeks sleeping, eating and playing—and reacting instinctively to much of what he or she sees, hears and smells. Toward the end of that seventh week, the pup's brain begins clicking and she starts to think. The thinking doesn't amount to much, nor does it make her less helpless than she has been, but it does seem to make her more curious about the world and anxious to try new things.

At eight weeks, most pups are ready for their new homes, although a few days earlier or a few weeks later won't matter to your pooch or to you. What's important is the planning. The transition will be easier on you if you've made some advance preparations, easier on the pup if the long association with you begins in a reasonably calm atmosphere.

As canines go, the pup is just an innocent baby. Although much more active and talented than her human counterpart, most things still have to be done for the pup and other things must be placed out of her reach. Luckily, she does not have to be bottle- or spoon-fed. Her meal is placed in a dish, the dish is placed on the floor, and the pup dives into the offering. Since the diving is often accompanied with from two to four paws, it is wise to give some advance thought to the dinner dish. It should not be easy to break, move or tip, and should be just deep enough to keep the food from spilling. If the family cook can't suggest and loan something, buy a metal dog dish, available in many sizes. You will also need a bowl or pan for the dog's drinking water.

The pup will need a place to sleep, of course, and the site should not be of the dog's own choosing until well after he's housebroken, which is never an instant miracle. Strictly speaking, the trick is to keep the pup confined to sleeping quarters so that she will not forget her toilet manners during the night. By nature, the canine is high on cleanliness, but a pup learns that the hard way. Until then, the owner must forgive and forget.

Puppies need to sleep safely and soundly in a site free from drafts, so pick the site before the dog arrives. While a pup can sleep in or on anything (box, pillow, your bed), the very best choice is a dog crate. Metal, wood and wire bench crates are all available in the marketplace, and it's always possible to make a wood crate at home, if you're handy with tools. During the day, the door to the crate is left open, so that the pup can enter for rest and sleep at will. At night, she sleeps in the crate with the door shut. More about crates later.

The only other problem over the first few days concerns the pup's personal freedom. When she is outdoors, she should be supervised at all times. Indoors, most rooms should be off limits, for not even the pup knows just when she'll be inspired to leave an unwelcome reminder of her presence on the floor. So one room, such as the kitchen, is enough. If that is inconvenient, a child's playpen set up in the corner of a room is big enough for most breeds.

Once those preparations are out of the way, you are ready for the pup's arrival. While the sooner the better may be your only thought on the matter, try to pick a date when there's a minimum of excitement on the home front. The less confusion, the better the pup's adjustment. Just the normal activities of everyday family life will be enough at first, and there's no need to rush the introduction of all your friends and relatives. This holds true for

Christmas, of course, whether the pup is an outright gift or a reward for brushing your teeth and polishing your shoes every day for ten months.

## Feeding

Whenever that day of arrival, the pup will expect his first meal on schedule. Since a sudden change of diet is a sure way to unforgettable, unwanted diarrhea, stay with the formula and schedule the pup has been following for at least the first two weeks. Most breeders wouldn't think of sending a pup to a new home without a couple of days' worth of free rations, and all will send you home with instructions. But no matter what recommended brand(s) of food come with your dog, the tried-and-true schedule for feeding an eight-week-old pup is four times a day. Another matter for consideration: if you won't be home at all the scheduled times, who'll do the feeding?

You may decide that the breeder's choice of Brand A is ridiculous and that a switch to Brand Z would be best for the pup. When the time comes, the changeover should be gradual and at a rate not exceeding 20 percent per day. Thus, on the first day of the change, the pup's food should be 80 percent Brand A and 20 percent Brand Z, and on the third day, it's 40 percent Brand A, 60 percent Brand Z; and on the fifth day it's 100 percent Brand Z. If loose stools or diarrhea occur along the way, go back to the prior day's ratio and proceed with the change at a smaller increase of Z per day. Then, if the pup doesn't return to normal, Z may be a great food for all other pups, but not yours. Try a brand of equal nutritional value. Fortunately, you have a big choice.

Wherever you find dog food for sale, you'll find an amazing number of brands on display. Usually, the bigger the retail store, the more brands, but even small stores give the buyer a choice between good and unworthy foods, and often the best costs less than the worst. To discover what's good and what isn't among the brands requires a little knowledge, the ability to read and the willingness to forget advertising, sales gimmicks and rumors.

Any canine, pup or adult, owes his or her good looks and vitality to eating the requisite amounts of protein, fat, carbohydrates, vitamins, minerals and water. It would be difficult to find a commercial dog food that did not have the right amount of carbohydrates, vitamins and minerals. As for water, what you drink is good for your dog (served at room temperature). Also, both dry and wet foods contain moisture; so you just can't avoid buying water (moisture) in dog foods. Normally, there is about 12 percent in dry foods (kibble) and 75 percent in wet (canned) foods.

The important ingredients are protein and fat. As for the latter, 6 percent is the minimum requirement, but some brands fall short of that. And many brands come up short on protein minimums: 25 percent for growing pups, 20 percent for adults.

To find out a brand's contents, study the label. There, if the pet food company is obeying the law, you will find a guaranteed analysis of the contents and a listing of the ingredients in order of quantity. The analysis will give the percentages of protein and fat. If those two counts satisfy you, go to the fine print of the listing and study the actual ingredients. Dogs utilize both animal and vegetable protein, although animal protein is more digestible. One or more of the first three ingredients should be meat, meat byproducts or bone meal. At least one cereal grain should be listed in no lower than sixth place.

While there are now semimoist dog foods around in abundance, dry and wet foods remain the big sellers. For many inexperienced dog owners, canned foods are the most popular. There can be no doubt about their convenience, and hardly any about their high cost, since just a little food is swimming in so much water. The protein count on a can, by the way, can be misleading. It is usually below 10 percent, but (for planning a diet) the true count is triple. If you removed the water, the percentages of the solid food contents would shoot up.

Any veteran dog owner will tell you that dry food is always the economy buy, and more so when you can buy in quantity, or fifty-pound sacks. Of course, a sack is not always convenient to store, but my easy solution has been twenty-gallon, galvanized garbage cans. If they are kept in a dry place, the temperature doesn't matter, and one container will hold fifty pounds with ease.

Dry food is not really designed to be served dry. For a pup, it is soaked in water until reasonably soft—about fifteen minutes. Most dog lovers believe that there must be something wrong with a meal that's as easy to prepare as a TV dinner, so they add a few ingredients. For flavor and protein, they will add a little meat. This can be raw or cooked; however, pork and fish should always be cooked, and fish and fowl should be cooked and boneless. For good canine bone, calcium lactate is added in the form of milk: dry milk is cheapest and it is sprinkled on the food before soaking. And, more for people who worry than for their dogs, the marketplace is loaded with expensive food supplements for pups. You *can* overdo a good thing: a pup is a very good thing, so try to resist costly temptations to stuff the little beast with goodies.

## Five-Day Program

As a pup moves along in life, he consumes more food per day but dines less frequently. During this process, from week to week, he gains pounds with rapidity, and the danger of overweight is always present. Since not even two littermates will grow at the same rate, it's impossible for the breeder to tell you just how much more food your pup will require from week to week. It's not as easy as simply increasing the daily ration by two cups of food every seven days. Still, judging the proper increase is not a great problem, and it won't be any problem if you adopt my Five-Day Program for diet efficiency.

This simple, safe, sane program is based on sight, touch and the sound belief that a healthy canine is a lean canine. Since dogs don't know when to stop eating and most owners confuse overfeeding with kindness, most dogs are fat. This is even more unhealthy than being underweight, which is unhealthy enough.

In the case of a short-coated dog, it's possible to judge whether a pup is at the proper weight just by look. If the ribs protrude, he's underweight and the daily ration should be increased. If you can't see the ribs and he's roundish, he's overweight and the daily ration needs to be cut. For a long-coated pup, if you can see a faint impression of the ribs or feel the ribs without an intervening layer of flesh, your pup is lean, or just right, and the daily ration needs only a slight increase. Judgment of a long-coated pup's weight depends on your touch. These checkups should be made once every five days.

While this method alone does not guarantee that your pup will always be lean during the important span of growth, it holds the promise that he'll be lean most of the time. After all, a few days and ounces over or under proper weight aren't going to damage him.

Most of the time, then, you'll be increasing the daily ration a little every five days. How much food a *little* represents will be an "almost" amount rather than a precise one. The amount cannot be precise because your pup will not only grow at his own pace, but the pace will vary from week to week, from month to month. The only thing that you can be sure about is that he is growing and his weight should increase from week to week. When this doesn't happen, suspect that something is wrong. If nothing else, either the pup is not digesting properly or the diet is inadequate. If two weeks go by without a change in weight, be sure that something is wrong and visit the vet.

The only way to really know your pup's weight from week to week, of course, is to actually weigh him. The quick, easy way to do this is to step on the scales twice—once with him in your arms and once without him. Subtract the without from the with, and you have the pup's weight.

Feeding Schedules

Sometimes it seems that there are more "absolutely the best" feeding schedules for pups than there are breeds of dogs. Every breeder has a favorite, and it's safe to rely on one recommended by any veteran hobby breeder. Some of the schedules are very precise as to days or weeks, and while there's nothing wrong with that except possible inconvenience or feeling guilty when one forgets, I prefer my own About Feeding Plan. It has never threatened the health or stunted the growth of any of my pups, and your pup will thrive on it whether you follow the changes right on the nose, or about a week one way or the other.

## About Feeding Plan
Up to 11 weeks, feed 4 times per day
11 to 20 weeks, feed 3 times per day
20 to 40 weeks, feed 2 times per day
After 40 weeks, 1 time per day

To keep the pup from begging or moaning about the way he's being deprived, it's possible to con him into one meal less per day by decreasing the amount of one feeding. For example, if you plan on going from three times to two times on Saturday, start lessening, a few days earlier, the size of the middle meal and increasing the size of the first and third meals. Change a little more each day, so that by Friday the middle meal is only a snack or a dog biscuit.

For the pup who won't forget, a dog biscuit is also a good substitute for the second meal when you are cutting back to one meal at forty weeks. For the pup who absolutely refuses to quiet down until he's had a fair-sized second meal, fool him with a dish of cooked vegetables. Except for the cabbage family, just about anything is okay, and the same goes for fresh fruit. Both are mostly water and nutritionally insignificant; they do not add weight, but they'll satisfy the hunger of a pup.

Once he gets down to one meal a day, the average dog will thrive on the schedule. For his sake, and for yours—if you would rather avoid his pestering—the meal should be served at about the same time every day. Most of the year on this hill, we feed the once-a-day dogs in the morning. But when nights get below forty and toward freezing, and all through the winter, the outdoor (kennel) dogs are fed in the late afternoon. When it's cold, who wants to sleep on an empty stomach? And since any warm-blooded animal expends more energy when it's cold, the outdoor dogs get bigger-than-normal meals in winter, plus a biscuit in the morning. We do not tell the indoor (house) dogs about the biscuit. If we did, there would be no peace.

## Housebreaking

Once you and your pup survive the first few days of your new relationship, the pooch is ready to start learning the routine that will lead to the gold medal in good manners and win the love of all the people under the same roof. This matter of housebreaking a pup is more a matter of conning or tricking than training. The pup is too young to rationalize or distinguish right from wrong, but his natural instincts are ready to be channeled to the owner's advantage. Consider the fact that it is quite natural for the pup to wet or unload when the moment is right, and he performs without thought about the deed or respect for the rug, your lap or wherever. To con him into performing in a more sanitary setting, such as the great outdoors (or on paper, if he's to be paper-trained), it is only necessary to know what he does not know— when the right moment is going to occur.

Happily, the right moments are not secrets. If wise old dogs could speak, they'd tell you that those moments occur when a pup awakens (from a nap or sleep), after he dines or drinks, after a little running and exercising, and after even a short play-session with you. Those are the times when an intelligent owner swings into immediate action: rush the pup to the great outdoors and stay there with him until the mission is accomplished, then pet and praise him and bring him back indoors. If the owner has an above-average IQ, he or she will do the same just before hitting the bed at night and just after jumping out in the morning.

The very thought of all those fast trips with the pup may

discourage you, but it is both the very best and the speediest method for housebreaking a new pup. By the third or fourth day, and sometimes earlier, going outdoors to relieve himself has become rote or almost instinctive, and the pup actually begins to cooperate and telegraph warnings that he's about ready to go. He does this in little ways: standing silently at the door, standing there or anywhere and whimpering or barking, circling a spot on the floor, scratching on a rug or in a corner, sniffing the hearth, or assuming the proper position for action. If you read those signs correctly and react as previously recommended, your pup will be housebroken, or almost so, very quickly.

*Almost so,* because we have been dealing with a young pup's day, more or less, and there is still the long night. During the course of an average, unexciting day, a healthy pup can keep under control for an hour or so and, as he grows older, for two hours. So if he's not going to get outdoors while you're asleep, it's a lead-pipe cinch that he can't contain himself for six or eight hours. Accidents are bound to happen.

There's no way to prevent those accidents, but you can minimize them by paying attention to a couple of small details that are generally overlooked by puppy owners. First, make it easy on the pup by sending him to bed as empty as possible. The last meal should be no closer to bedtime than four hours, the last drink (small) three hours, and the last visit outdoors just prior to lights out. Then, confine the pup to his crate, and get him outdoors again as soon as he stirs in the morning. During the first week, there may be an accident or two, but there may not be any during the second week, and there should not be any by the end of the third.

Figure on a little over two weeks for nightbreaking, and a little over one week for daybreaking. The weeks run concurrently, of course, so anybody should be able to completely housebreak a pup in two weeks, give or take a few days—and often it takes less than a week. And let's not forget that once housebroken, a pup stays that way only with owner cooperation. The newcomer must get outdoors every couple of hours—whether he makes telltale signs or not—until he's six months old. Don't lock him in the kitchen and go to the movies and come home and expect to find the floor in immaculate shape.

## Dog Crates

While a dog crate is hardly indispensable, it is one of the handiest inventions credited to dogdom. Of the many ways to nightbreak a pup, I've found the crate-training method to be the best of all, and the quickest. You can build a crate or buy one. If you buy, the most practical type is known as the folding wire-bench crate. When it is not in use, the crate can be folded and stored. For moving, it rides well folded and tied to a carrier atop a car, or fits set up in the back of a station wagon. A dog is always a heck of a lot safer riding in a crate: it keeps him from being tossed about and prevents him from sticking his head out the window to sniff the very breezes that may blow damaging particles into his eyes.

Since the floor of a wire crate is usually galvanized metal and hardly comfortable, a wooden floor (of ½-inch exterior plywood) can be cut to size. This is covered with a thick layer of newspapers for nightbreaking. Later the completely housebroken pup might continue to use the crate for sleeping quarters. Around here, my wife makes a simple cedar mattress for the crate. This amounts to a pillow slip made from tough mattress ticking. The slip is stuffed with cedar ribbons, then sewn closed. Outdoors, the kennel dogs also sleep on cedar ribbons. If a dog snoozes on cedar, you never have to worry about fleas.

A crate has many extra advantages. It's a great place to stuff a dog when you must get him out of the way, as when rich Uncle Archibald, the famous dog hater, visits on Christmas. And it makes it possible to take your pet along on almost any trip, since it will satisfy the fussiest managers of motels and those curious friends who adore dogs but hate to see dog hairs in every room. If it doesn't mean bankruptcy, a crate is a sound investment for a dog owner. For a Golden Retriever, figure on it costing about forty dollars. If you buy rather than build, select a size that will permit your pup (when an adult) room for lying and sitting, but not standing.

A crate is not necessary for nightbreaking, but it does hurry the process and keeps the premises more sanitary. Without it, the thing to keep in mind is that the pup is not going to get through the night without mishaps. Prayers won't alter that fact, nor will lectures. Still, you can keep the number of accidents down by taking the dog outdoors just prior to bedtime and watching the food and drink intake, as prescribed, before that. Then, before stowing the pup away in the place where he's to spend the night, minimize the chances of yowls in the dark by providing him with some company. A pup resents being alone more than a baby does, but will usually accept sounds as company, and a low-playing radio or a loud-ticking clock near his bed (but out of his reach) often suffices. A couple of night activists such as hamsters running on a wheel are ideal for soothing a pup. The continuing sound will put him to sleep, and the more he sleeps, the fewer his mishaps.

## Training

The urge to teach a pup many things in a rush is understandable, forgivable and a mistake. Whatever the age of the baby canine, it takes her awhile to settle down in the new environment, and the settling will be prolonged if she is expected to learn too much. So be pleasantly surprised if you can housebreak her within two weeks, and buy yourself a present if you can do it in one week.

During this transition period from a pup in the raw to a pup with clean habits, the new pet can also be conned into learning a few other things that will be of help to both of you in the future. This is a very convenient time for the dog to become accustomed to her call (pet) name. In the dog fancy's higher echelons, selecting the right name is not a simple matter. Rather, it is both art and science; many worthy essays and several books have been written on the subject, and lists of appropriate names for both canine sexes are available in return for small sums.

However, on these pages, naming is regarded as a simple matter. The choice is yours, the pup won't care, and the way you spell it is unimportant. You will find a couple of points worth considering, however: a short name with no more than two syllables will be easy to shout and kind to your lungs; and to avoid confusion, the sound of the name should not be similar to the sound of a command word. For example, *Stan* and *David* and *Judy* and *Dawn* are easy to shout, but forget *Stan* and *Dawn* because to a pup's ears they will sound like *stand* and *down*.

So your new pup's name is Judy? She doesn't understand a word of English, but she'll associate the sound of Judy with herself if you use it often and correctly. On the first day, or on whatever day you decide on the name, use *Judy* whenever you talk to her, and always use *Judy* first. Wrong: "You're a good girl, Judy," and "Come and get it, Judy." Right: "Judy, you're a good girl," and "Judy, come and get it." Get her attention first, not after you've said something. Otherwise you might as well be talking to the nearest lamp shade. This name-first policy also helps prepare the pup for basic training.

## Collars and Leashes

When you are playing with Judy during the first couple of weeks, you might as well con her into a couple of musts about the future: collar and leash. Some pups toss fits about wearing a collar and others are totally unconcerned, but the average pup fusses a little for a few days and then forgets about it, so long as she's not forced to wear the damn thing day and night. A few times a day, slip the collar around Judy's neck for several minutes, and before she's housebroken, she'll consider herself undressed without it.

About collars. They come in a dazzling array of colors, shapes and styles, and are fashioned from leather, chain or fabric. While the great majority are overpriced, impractical and easy to find, a few worthy ones are still being manufactured and worth the hunt. Of the worthies, the best one for most dogs (pups and adults) is the nylon choke, still no more than a dollar and change at most retail outlets. It comes in a variety of colors and sizes and is washable.

*Choke* is an unfortunate name for the collar and may be the reason why many dog lovers avoid trying it on their dogs. I prefer calling it a slip collar (and will henceforth), since it justs slips over the dog's head and ears and hangs a little loose when it's the proper size.

On display in the store, a slip collar doesn't look like a collar. It's just a length of cord with a metal ring attached at each end. By pushing the cord through either ring, a loop is formed and becomes the collar. A tug on the ring at the end of the loop will tighten it. This makes the slip collar ideal for training as well as for everyday wear: a slight tug on the leash causes a slight tightening of the collar that is felt by the wearer. Yes, the pooch feels a pressure, but it doesn't hurt—it certainly doesn't choke, and the action should not be confused with cruelty.

The slip collar that fits a pup will be too small for him in a few months and impossibly small when he's an adult. So be prepared to buy more than one and probably three in the first year, and be happy that the total cost is less than the chain or leather collars that you might have purchased. Chain and leather will damage the coat, are often heavy and bulky and are far too strong for almost every dog and any pup. Canines are not wild beasts. They have been domesticated, but some dog lovers act as if they don't believe that fact.

When it comes to practical leashes, the best one around is still an economy item, selling for about $1.50. It is called a work lead, is made of webbed canvas, comes in dull greens and tans and can't be beat for durability. The lead is usually a half-inch wide and comes in several lengths, but the six-footer (including hand loop and metal snap) is probably the most practical for any pup or dog.

Getting a pup accustomed to a lead (leash) can be a big problem, and if the problem continues, it can disrupt an otherwise happy relationship. A baby canine can't be expected to understand the rationale of the long thing and is almost sure to fight it—if you try to make him accept it at first glance (or wear). On the other hand, it's easy to con any pup into accepting the inconvenience.

Along about the time a pup has worn a collar without complaint for a couple of days, toss the lead on the floor and let her play with it for ten minutes or so. On the next day, snap the lead to her collar and let her drag it around at will. The following day, do likewise and also pick up your end of the lead and join the fun, but don't attempt to persuade her to do anything. Finally, on the fourth day, put the pup on the lead and take her for an uncontrolled walk. Repeat for two days.

*Uncontrolled?* Yes, in the sense that one of you will be the leader and the other the follower, and your roles will probably interchange every ten feet. Indoors or out, pick a safe place for your walks, so that you won't have to keep your pup on a tight lead.

Now, whatever her age, if the pup more or less knows her call name, seems to wear the collar with equanimity and doesn't hate the lead, guess what? She is ready for the plain training that will make her a pleasure to own.

Labrador pups at six weeks. Their sire was a black and their dam was a yellow. Courtesy of the Tom Phillips, owner-breeders, Ro-Shan Kennels, Canada.

Dalmatian pup at eight weeks with almost all of his spots already in place. Courtesy of the owner, Janet Ashbey.

Smooth Collie pup *(left)* at fourteen weeks, courtesy of Mrs. M. Burrell, Braemar Kennels, Canada. The Rough Collie pup on the jacket is seven weeks old and was bred by Gail P. Jones. Both pups are tri-colors. Chow Chow *(right)* at four months, courtesy of F.P.A. Odenkirchen, Mi-Pao Kennels, Canada.

Keeshonds at nine weeks, courtesy of Mrs. Virginia Ruttkay, Ruttkay Kennels.

Finnish Spitz pup (*left*) at eight weeks. Owner, Bette Isacoff. (*Mrs. M. Koehler*) Bouviers des Flandres (*right*) still wear their natural ears at six weeks of age. This trio came from Madrome Lodge Kennels. (*Brooks*)

Norwegian Elkhound pups at eight weeks. Courtesy of Vin-Melca Kennels. (*Ludwig*)

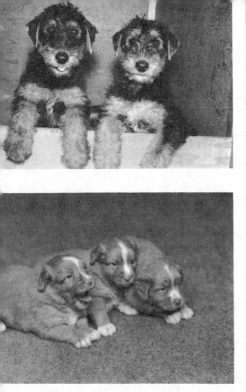

Airedale Terrier pups *(top left)* at nine weeks, courtesy of the Hugh S. Andrews, Jolabar Kennels. Nova Scotia Duck Tolling Retriever pups *(left),* of Sundrummer Kennels, at seven weeks of age. *(Aurora Studio Ltd.)* Otterhound pup (*right*) at ten weeks, courtesy of Cragmont Kennels. (Jayne *Langdon)* Siberian Husky pups *(below)*—these, of Monadnock Kennels— know what a chow line is by the time they are six weeks old.

# 6

# The Plain Training of Frolicsome Harry

Plain training is called basic training by conformists, since it does cover the simple commands any canine pet should know and obey if he's to be more of a companion than a nuisance. So a pup's familiarity with the five basic commands, and proper reactions to them, are important, whether the pooch is a purebred or an Americanis. In most cases, the timing of the dog's response—immediate or delayed—is unimportant, so long as he gets around to obeying the command and pleasing his owner before the sun sets. But in the case of a purebred, one good enough for the breed ring, smart enough for the Obedience trial, or both, the responses must be honed or the going will be rough at the dog shows.

The five basics—*come*, *heel*, *sit*, *down* and *stay*—can be taught in any order, but on these pages we'll deal with them in the order named. While there is nothing difficult about teaching them to even the stupidest dog, a great many dog lovers can't seem to get the hang of it. It would be difficult to prove that any of them are dimwits, but some are certainly easy marks for the dog world's newest careerists—consultants who collect handsome fees for their sometimes strange advice.

Teaching, training, or conning your pup—take your choice—doesn't require much in the way of skill, but it does require enthusiasm. If you have developed a cool, casual image for yourself, forget it during training sessions. These should be fun times for both you and the pup, and the more you clown, the easier the task. And then there are these five nuggets for each of the five basic commands:

1. Timing. Short training periods, several times a day, are best. The younger the pup, the briefer the attention span, and it's useless to continue after he's lost interest. At ten or eleven weeks, a pup will be able to study for five minutes, three or four times a day. Just when depends on your own free time, but I prefer just before a pup's meals, when he's hungry and alert. The tidbits he gets as rewards don't dim his appetite and do encourage his eagerness to please.

2. Setting. The training site does not have to be constant (indoors, outdoors, basement, garage, etc.) so long as it is devoid of major distractions such as loud noises, strong scents, unrelated actions and curious people. You and your voice are important, nothing else. The only other person who should be present (as a silent observer) is the member of your family who would act as a substitute trainer in your absence and employ the same methods. A pup can only take one trainer at a time and two overall.

3. Continuity. Train the pup every day until he has the five commands down pat on a more-or-less basis. But don't train when you are at odds with the world or not feeling well or in a big hurry—all times when you are likely to be impatient, sound sour, and discourage and confuse the student. If you con the pup into believing that you are greater than you really are, then he'll be eager to please. When you do take a day off, you set back the training program at least two days.

4. Vocalizing. Your voice is more important to the pup than your looks, dress or reputation. A loud, authoritative tone is wrong, and so is a whispery, saccharine one. Just right is a conversational tone that is pleasantly firm, designed to leave the impression that you mean business but will not shoot if the response is inadequate. It is a tricky vocal quality to achieve, but

rehearsals bring results, and a walk in the woods to command trees is permissible. In giving commands, always use a firm tone that's short of scary. Reserve the sweet talk for when the mission is accomplished. That's the time for praise and reward.

5. Progressing. If the pup is taught to obey one command at a time, success is inevitable; otherwise, confusion is a certainty. Thus, he should learn to come on command and carry it out almost all of the time, before he progresses to heeling and then to sitting and so on. While it is impossible to predict even roughly the number of days or weeks it takes for an average pup to learn all five basic commands, it is sometimes reassuring to know that most pups are natural time-savers and will learn the next command faster than the present one.

If you have faith in these five nuggets, or just enough belief to try them, you'll cut training time down to the minimum. Of course, you'll also need a pup and these three training tools: (1) a slip collar; (2) a work lead; and (3) a half-dozen tidbits, such as pieces of kibble, bite-size shredded wheat or small squares of dried liver.

Here's how Harry the housebroken pup is trained around here.

## "Harry, come!"

The pup knows his name just from hearing it often, so he doesn't look blank when he hears the name—unless the words run into each other so that they sound like one, or Harikum. For best results—for *any* results—speak distinctly and a pause slightly between words.

In all truth, Harry doesn't have to be taught this command if he has been conned into responding during the transition period (Chapter Five). The conning begins after he knows his name, and a convenient time is when his meals are served. Sing out, "Harry, come!" as the dish hits the floor. Do likewise at odd moments, such as when you want him to come to where you're sitting, and praise him when he responds. If he does not, don't let him off the hook, but lure him to you in some fashion, by clapping your hands, rolling on the floor, making odd noises or waving a turkey leg. Use your ingenuity, but attract him in some way without using force. Then, even if it takes an hour, be sure to praise him. He'll learn to come on command by rote.

Should your pup resist all forms of trickery and foolishness, it's best to suspect that he needs a little more aging before tackling this command. He should handle it with ease after he's learned the *sit* and *stay*, commands that will be found up ahead. Please wait.

## "Harry, heel!"

Again, this shouldn't be a problem if, during the transition period, your pup has become accustomed to the collar and lead, and you've taken him for a few walks.

When at heel, a dog remains at your left side whatever your speed (walking, running) or nonspeed (standing still). Even if you are left-handed, the left side is always correct, although it really doesn't make any difference if you prefer your right side, unless, of course, you intend to enter your beloved in competition at dog shows, where etiquette demands the left side. That's considered sufficient reason for limiting what appears below to left-handed advice. Just switch hands if you prefer the right side.

*At your left side* means that the dog is even with you, not lagging behind or bouncing ahead, and close enough for you to grab him by the collar without his body pressing against your leg. He should not jump on you or anybody else, or cause you to stumble or chase a passing cat. You train him to avoid such antics by controlling him; your control is the lead and your control point is your left hand. If you use the recommended work lead, you'll find it inconveniently long for this command. Solve this by holding the excess of the lead in your right hand; then string it across to your left hand, then down to the pup's collar.

Ready? The pup is at your left, standing or sitting, and his lead is attached. Now, simultaneously step off on your left foot, utter the magic words, "Harry, heel!" and give a little yank. The yank is always accompanied by the command words and later is used only to correct the student when he lags or surges ahead or takes a different direction from you.

The only problem for you is a small one: how tight should the lead be? That portion of it running from the pup's collar to your left hand should be a little loose: not so tight that the pup can't lower his head, and not so loose that he won't really feel the yanks; so experiment. Although he won't know it, the big problem for the pup is your overconfidence. Chances are that you'll figure he's a polished, trusted performer much too soon, and you'll try keeping him at heel off lead. Please don't try that in public. It'll be a long, long time before he realizes that trucks, cars, big dogs and strangers are not always good friends.

## "Harry, sit!"

This is another easy command to teach a pup without him being aware of what's happening. A handy time to begin is after he seems to know his name and will respond to the meal call. When he arrives on the scene, hold his filled dinner dish above his head and keep giving him the sit command until he sits. When he does, praise him and serve the meal.

You can be sure that the pup will sit, and sooner than you think. He'll get tired of looking up and discover that it's easier to do so while sitting. After a few days, help your cause along by offering him a tidbit between meals now and again, but always make the treat a reward for his proper response to the command.

For the recalcitrant pup, it's back to the collar and lead and scheduled training sessions. The pup stands at your left and you turn toward him. This time, your left hand is free, and the lead is held taut and short in your right hand. Hold it about two feet above the pup's head.

When you give the command, the pup might sit. This does

happen, either by accident or because he feels you want him to do something and sitting is easy. If he obeys the command, heap lavish praise on his brow and send thanks to Saint Francis of Assisi. You have a natural sitter and you're lucky.

When the pup does not sit on command, use your left hand to push down on his rump as you repeat the words. When that doesn't work, as in the case of an extremely obstinate canine, keep pushing and use your right hand to pull up on the lead. Unless you are a weakling, or at least considerably weaker than the pup, he must sit.

Once the pup starts sitting on command, it's a pretty convenient time to teach him to sit properly—especially if you have Obedience plans for him. In the sport of Obedience, the dog loses points for a sloppy sit. The correct sitting posture is defined as a square sit: the dog's forelegs drop straight from the shoulders, his rump is planted between closely tucked hindlegs and the body does not twist or lean. Like most people, most dogs sit unattractively, but it's easy to correct in the puppy stage.

Keep the pup on lead. When he assumes a sloppy sit, correct him by moving his legs with your hands. Next, move him ahead at heel, put him on a sit and correct him whenever it is necessary. Whenever he does sit properly, bestow praise and reward. (If he barks when you sit, correct your own slouch.)

## "Harry, stay!"

Pups are not very adept at interpreting hand signals, but most of them have no trouble with this one. It can be taught with or after the verbal command. Try it with collar but without lead.

First, put the pup on your left side on a sit. The object is to keep him there while you move a few feet. As you utter the *stay* command, step ahead and swing your left arm back so that your open palm almost touches the pup's nose. If the pup fails to realize that your palm is a stop sign, he'll attempt to follow you. Grab his collar, restrain him, put him back on a sit and try again. Once he learns to stay at five feet, try him at ten and then twenty and so on. When he stays at twenty feet, he should be able to obey either the vocal or the hand command, and you might try dropping the words.

It's only human to expect too much from a pup, so beware with this command. Don't expect a pup under six months old to remain on a stay for as long as a minute. A well-trained adult can hardly stand the strain for three minutes. And it's only fair to warn you that this one basic command may take longer to get across to the canine than all the others combined. Happily, the stay command is really worth the effort. You'll probably use it more than any other on a normal day, just to keep the bundle of energy out of trouble.

When he is comfortable with the *stay* ritual, even the most stubborn pup is ripe for learning the *come* command. Put him on a sit and stay, move off ten feet, turn and sing out with the "Harry, come!" and the pup will come. Your words act as a release.

If yours is the rare pup who won't come, use the foolish antics described earlier for this command. And if they don't work, this probably will:

Put the pup on a sit and attach the lead. Put him on a stay and as you move off, pay out the lead. At five feet, turn and give the come command. If that fails, repeat and add a yank. And if that fails, simply substitute hauling for the yank and force the pup to come to you. Failing everything, you'll just have to wait until your pup is old enough to take you seriously.

## "Harry, down!"

There are numerous ways of teaching this command, but the one with the least wear and tear on the teacher is presented here. It calls for collar and lead.

Put the pup on a sit and stay. Stand and face him and hold the lead loosely so that it loops to within two or three inches of the floor. Now, on the command, simply step on the lead. The pup will feel pressure on his neck and go down. He won't be hurt, but he will be surprised, and kind words will reassure him. Repeat until he goes down without pressure on the lead. The method usually gets results in fewer than a dozen enforced descents to the floor.

Well, those are the basic commands—almost. There's also the *stand* command, generally considered as a sixth basic for purebreds and optional for all other canines. Since every dog with four normal legs knows how to stand, the command may seem pointless, but it really means that the dog should stand properly or in a stance that shows him off at his best. With a few exceptions (Bulldog, Basset Hound, Bedlington Terrier, all Setters, German Shepherd Dog, Pekingese, Welsh Corgi), almost all the purebreds stand properly with head up, topline (back) level, forelegs dropping straight down, feet pointed straight ahead and hind legs planted a little wide with hocks straight. Each breed standard specifies the ways the ears and tail should be held.

For the sake of anatomy and good health, it would be nice if all dogs stood properly—or at least as we think they should—but that's not the case, although there are probably more standers per capita among canines than people, it is easier to con a dog than to bribe a person into an attractive stance.

On this mountain top, the conning usually begins along about the time a pup is at peace with the *stay* command. For human comfort and convenience, the pup is lifted and placed on a steady, nonskid surface—the top of a solid crate, table or workbench is dandy—during intervals devoted to nail clipping, grooming, removing ticks or burrs from coat and checking eyes and ears and anything else. Whatever the reason for placing him above ground level, he is told to.stand and at least one eagle eye is kept on him so that he can be prevented from sitting or falling. The word *stand* is used constantly, and if mother nature hasn't taught him the proper stance, his limbs are moved into the proper position. Lift the forelegs by the elbows and correct, and lift the hind legs by the hocks.

Naturally, or after many corrections, the pup who stands properly on high won't do so for very long before moving a leg, twisting his back, turning his head for a view of the rear or shifting his balance. So after he goes fifteen seconds without ruining his stance, it's high time to incorporate the *stay* command. Thus, the *Harry, stand!* becomes *Harry, stand (pause) stay!* When he holds a stand for thirty seconds without moving more than one leg, the pup is ready for a few practice sessions on the good earth.

Collar and lead are useful at ground level. Just move the pup along at heel and use the *stand* command when you halt. The lead is used to keep the pup's head up and away from sniffing the ground while both on the move and standing. A slight upward yank does the trick. And if the stance is wrong, a tug moves the pup ahead a few steps and he often corrects himself. If not, it's back to correcting by hand.

If canines have a point of view, they probably consider the *stand* command to be a product of human silliness. They could be right most of the time. It is only a must command for show dogs, Obedience dogs and dogs posing for oil portraits. Otherwise, it isn't used much in the average dog lover's home and it doesn't really help a pooch become a better pet.

As for all the six, or just the five basic, commands, a dog is never too old to learn them, although the older he is, the longer the learning usually takes. Insofar as puppyhood goes, the most difficult training time is during a canine's fourth month, when the baby teeth are being forced out and are replaced by the permanent dentition (20 uppers, 22 lowers). Some pups are understandably irritable for a few weeks and not exactly keen about adding to their knowledge. It's a good time to slow down the training pace, or to confine the activity to rehearsing and polishing the things the pup already knows. If he's not doing something, his obedience will diminish and it'll be rough getting him back into a responsive mood.

It doesn't make an iota of difference whether you teach a pup the commands in English, French, German, Italian or a language of your own invention (*come, venir, kommen, venire, collit*), just so long as every command word is consistent. Through repetition, the pup relates sounds to actions. Thus, if you want to impress your friends, you can train your pet to obey commands in several languages (one command per language), or you can startle just about anyone by training your dog to sit on *fly*, go down on *jump*, and come on *eat a banana*. A little inventiveness can make training sessions what they really should be—fun for both you and your dog.

## Obedience Schools

The pup who knows the basic commands is socially acceptable almost anywhere and often even wins the hearts of dog haters. As previously explained, it does not take genius to train (con) a dog, but that does not alter the fact that many sincere dog lovers just can't get anywhere with their beloved canines. If that's the case with you, don't despair and don't run for the nearest psychiatrist. Instead, look around for the nearest obedience training school, where owners are taught how to train and handle their dogs, but *en masse* rather than privately. Since several thousand of these schools now dot our land, it's reasonable to assume that tens of thousands of dog lovers per year find it either impossible, inconvenient or plain frustrating to teach the basic commands or anything else to their dogs. Almost all achieve success through what amounts to group therapy at one of the obedience schools. Some schools are better than others, of course, but one that has been around for more than five years must have something going for it, including satisfied patrons and their trained dogs. The schools are sponsored by kennel clubs and civic organizations, and others are the side-business enterprises of professional trainers.

An average course runs eight to ten weeks for one early-evening hour per week, and classes are limited to about ten owners and their dogs. Whenever it is possible, dogs are pretty much restricted to the same age range per class: pups, senior pups or adults. The ages of the handlers, of course, are mixed. Average costs for a complete course run from a registration fee of a dollar or so (civic) to fifteen or twenty dollars (private).

## Manners

Unfortunately, not even schools teach canines the equivalents of good manners, and without them, the pup who dwells with a family becomes a pain in the neck. Any pup will develop unacceptable personal habits as the weeks move along. If they are not nipped in the bud, these habits will become part of the pooch's life-style. Short of giving away such a dog, the only recourse is to excuse the bad habits as cute ones. Show me a cute—or spoiled—dog, and I'll show you an inept owner who is willing to keep company on the pet's terms.

What are canine bad manners? The AKC doesn't object, but you and your parents might not approve of Harry's habit of emptying every wastebasket and spreading the contents. Under this roof, the house rules do not permit dogs (or small fry) to do that, to chew lamp cords or chair legs, to run off with towels or napkins, to eat rugs and pillows, to jump on sofas or chairs or beds or visitors, to pull on curtains or drapes, to beg at the table, to steal from the table, to borrow and digest books, to bark when the phone rings or to engage in rough-and-tumble play with each other.

The only way to teach good manners is by correcting bad manners and being timely about it. If the pup develops the habit of playing in the fireplace and then scattering cold ashes over the living-room floor, catch him in the act and correct him at once—not ten minutes from now, when he won't remember what the heck the correction is for. The longer you delay, the more his confusion and the less effective (if at all) the correction.

It is not difficult to convince a fun-loving pup that he's done something wrong. Simply hold, caution and impress: (1) grab him by the loose skin around the neck; (2) use a firm tone to deliver such words as "Bad dog, bad, bad, bad dog"; and (3) finish off with a whack on the little beggar's bottom. The grip is just strong enough to hold but not to hurt; there's no need to use his name—he knows you're talking to him; and the whack shouldn't drive him across the room—just strong enough to sting him. This correction is applied as often as needed until it is no longer needed.

Since bad habits do not appear on schedule, corrections are on a whenever basis and can begin as early as mistake times during housebreaking—but only if it's the pup who is really guilty, not a careless owner. A common human mistake or bad habit is expecting too much, such as perfection after one or two corrections for a wrongo. The pup will learn, but in time, not right now. Persistence does pay off. How often has somebody told you not to wear muddy shoes in the house?

Anyone capable of feeding a pup should be able to raise a mannerly pup, and that goes for even the unimaginative dog lover who fails to teach his beloved the basic commands. Again, it need not be the end of the world for the completely helpless dog owner. Such a person is not alone by a long shot and is always around in numbers large enough to keep the dog game's newest professionals laughing all the way to the bank. Known as canine psychologists, they are not, as the term suggest, dogs who probe into people problems, but people who consult on dog problems. As such, they are rays of hope for helpless dog lovers who can get up the fees. They have been known to solve problems, nobody talks about the failures, and the last one I met at a dog show reported this case history:

The dog was adorable, obedient, and completely housebroken, except for the dining room. My first advice was to keep the dog out of the dining room, but there were too many doors, so that was impractical. So I told the owner that she would have to think like a canine, and then when she corrected her dog, he would understand and realize that he'd done something wrong. I advised her to get down on her hands and knees and growl when the dog made a mistake.

Did that correction work? The expert was positive that it had, since the lady's check hadn't bounced and he had not heard from her since. But later, while chatting with her by phone, I learned that the growling had not worked and that she had sold the dog. Let's hope it was to somebody who lived in a house without a dining room. That woman, by the way, had great faith. She had just bought a new pup from a hobby breeder who is also a canine psychologist. Obviously, the latter has a sure thing going.

If you can't cure your pup of a particular bad habit, feel free to consult one of those self-appointed experts. But before doing so, think a few thrifty thoughts. Maybe you haven't been going more than halfway with your pooch, or you've been expecting too much or your impatience is showing. Or perhaps, just perhaps, owning a dog really isn't your cup of tea. You can be a dog lover and not a dog owner. That's not a disgrace.

# 7

# How to Become a Dog Fancier

Ownership or co-ownership of a purebred dog is essential for a dog lover who dreams of becoming a dog fancier. However, that's just a first step, and the dream remains unfulfilled until the lover-owner proves enthusiasm for the dog and the dog's breed. Becoming a hobby breeder is one way, but that's a lot of expensive trouble. It's much easier and less costly to enter the dog in competition at dog shows—breed ring, or Obedience trial, or both. There, the lover-owner wins immediate recognition as a dog fancier. If the fancier continues in either or both sports, he or she becomes more expert on the breed than most hobby breeders, a general rule that hardly anybody in the dog game disputes (the few exceptions being breeders).

Equal rights has never been a problem for dog fanciers, and the ratio of women to men is 3 to 1, girls to boys 2 to 1. There are many married teams; their offspring are often involved, and it is not unusual to run into three generations of one family pursuing their roles as dog fanciers at the same show.

Fanciers also come in most ages, or from those just old enough to control their dogs to senior citizens who still have a bounce in their steps. It's a little different for the dogs. Six months is their minimum age, either sex.

Discerning dog fanciers know that six months is too tender an age for most breeds to have a go at the shows, but wisdom often lags behind hopes. Very few of the wisest fanciers in the U.S. can wait for their purebred dogs to mature before rushing them into the sports. However, all know that they can't rush ahead with just any purebred. The only eligible breeds are the ones carrying the AKC stamp of approval as recognized or miscellaneous, and the individual dog must have a registered or listed number.

As anyone who became a dog fancier yesterday will tell you, there are two general types of genuine dog shows staged in the United States, and together they total about five thousand per year. The majority are *match shows*, regarded in the fancy as practice sessions or dress rehearsals for the events that really count—the *point shows*. There are now some sixteen hundred point shows. Most are *all-breed*, meaning that dogs of all AKC breeds are welcome, and the rest are *specialty* and limited to certain breeds, such as all the toy breeds or all the spaniel breeds or just one breed. What makes point shows so important is that they are the only places where a dog can win points toward his or her championship. No matter how great the dog is, it is impossible for a purebred to win a championship by staying at home.

These days, a big match show runs to 1,000 dogs and the big point shows run up to about 4,500. The former are always one-day events running from four to six hours. Most of the latter also run one day, but with longer hours. Both types of shows adhere to the rules and regulations of the AKC, but at the match shows, this adherence is casual and at the point shows, it's strict. At either type of show, the oldest sport—breed ring—is always present, and the youngest—Obedience—is much more in evidence than it was a decade ago.

When it comes down to the dog fancy's two major sports, the general public knows far more about breed ring showing, which has been around for more than a century. The rules are pretty much the same as they were fifty years ago, and the goal has remained constant: to find the very best dog present via a lengthy process of elimination that begins with purebred pups. Still, the average dog lover doesn't understand the workings of the elimination process, and the average A-student is not familiar with the championship point system. You are probably one or the other or both. Chances are that you own or will own a purebred, and that you might become a dog fancier and turn your pet into a champion, or you wouldn't be reading this page.

First things first. A dog is eligible for a try at the canine crown if he or she is old enough (at least 6 months) and a registered member in good standing of a recognized AKC breed. If the dog is a member of the AKC miscellaneous breed, and even if properly listed, he or she may be eligible for showing but cannot become a champion. Moral: if you want a champion, be darn sure the breed is a recognized one.

From the above, it would seem that any registered purebred of the right age can be shown. No, no. A dog is disqualified if:

1. He or she is vicious, lame, deaf, or totally blind.
2. He or she is not whole (normal). A bitch cannot be spayed. A male must have both testicles in the scrotum. (When buying a male pup, be sure testes are present; many breeders and most buyers don't check.)
3. He or she does not meet the general specifications of the breed standard. In some breeds, certain eye and coat colors, tail carriages, ear types and sizes are not permitted for show. In most breeds, cropped ears and docked tails are in violation of show rules, and the same goes for any other changes from the norm. (Before buying a purebred pup, study the breed standard and check the dog over for defects.)

Okay. When the dog is old enough, the purebred who passes those tests with flying colors is ready for the breed ring. Now the only problem is whether or not to show your pooch, and that depends pretty much on the dog's virtues, your determination, and a certain measure of luck.

Love alone does not make a champion. If that were true, all show dogs would become champions, whereas only about one in fifty does. It's not that all the dogs who fail are bums, but many worthy dogs are shown too early or not shown often enough or not handled to advantage.

In AKC territory, to become a champion, a dog must win a minimum of fifteen championship points, and the points must be won under no fewer than three different judges, and at least two of the wins must be majors. At a given point show, a dog can win up to five points, and a major win amounts to three, four or five points. Thus, the greatest purebred in the land can't win a title in fewer than three shows, and it might take him a long time and dozens of shows.

Generally—and there are only three exceptions—points are won in the classes at the breed level. The number of points up for grabs in each sex depends upon the number of class (nonchampionship) dogs and bitches in competition. For show purposes, males are dogs and females are bitches, and while they are granted equal opportunities at this level, they don't always compete for equal points. In some breeds, it takes more dogs than bitches to win five points, and in other breeds the reverse is true. So the point schedules can be different for each sex of a given breed, a fact that sometimes confuses spectators, but never dog fanciers. Nor are the latter bewildered by what might seem to be a grand incongruity: the point schedule is not the same for all breeds. This makes sense of course, since some breeds are more popular and abundant than others, and the popular ones are bound to attract larger turnouts. So the AKC in its wisdom might require forty-five Saint Bernard dogs for five points but only ten Chow Chows. At dog shows, minority breeds get a fair shake.

Dog fanciers don't have to memorize the point schedule for a given breed. At any point show, the current schedules for all recognized breeds appear in the show catalogue, the handy guide to all the purebreds in competition, along with times for judging and other pertinent information. For easy identification, each dog has a number, which appears on an armband worn by the dog's handler in the ring.

The use of the word *current* is important, for the point schedules are revised annually. The only other vital information about the schedules is that the AKC always has seven in operation: one for each of the four sectors of the continental forty-eight states, and one each for Alaska, Hawaii and Puerto Rico. Again, that's because of breed popularity, or lack of same. The Standard Poodle is very popular in California but not in Alaska, where the Alaskan Malamute is easy to find, and that breed is rare in Hawaii and Puerto Rico.

Whatever the breed, and no matter the predecided points for each sex of the breed, dogs are judged first. The winnowing begins by finding a first-place winner in each of five classes:

1. **Puppy.** Six to twelve months, whelped in the U.S. or Canada, and not a champion.
2. **Novice.** Six months and over, ditto for whelping. Can't compete after three wins in this class, or after winning one championship point or a first in any of following classes.
3. **Bred-by-Exhibitor.** Age as in Novice, whelped in the United States, and not a champion. Must be owned or co-owned by breeder or breeder's spouse and handled by breeder or a member of immediate family.
4. **American-bred.** Same age as above, whelped in the United States of a United States mating, and not a champion.
5. **Open.** Same age. This is the only class for dogs whelped overseas and dogs who are already champions. While

champs are rarely entered, it is the toughest class to win, since experienced show dogs (most with points to their credit) are usually found here.

After finding a winner in each class, the breed judge evaluates them and finds (in his or her opinion) the best of the lot. That one dog becomes Winners Dog (WD) and is awarded the allotted championship points for dogs of that breed. Then the judging is repeated for the bitches in each class, the victor is declared Winners Bitch (WB) and collects her points. These two, WD and WB, are the only survivors of the competition in the classes, and they proceed into the grand finale at the breed level:

**Best of Breed.** (Sometimes called *Best of Variety of Breed* (BOV), as would be the case in such breed varieties as Rough Collie and Smooth Collie.) With the exception of the two survivors, all the other competitors are champions of record. The big winner here is Best of Breed (BOB), for only he or she will continue at the next level of competition. The consolation prizes are Best of Opposite Sex (BOS) and Best of Winners (BW), and the latter is either WD or WB. The order of awards: BOB, BW, and BOS.

Of the three, only BOB proceeds onward and upward to the group level, where the competition is always much tougher. The BOB designates, each the best of his (or her) breed present on the day, have a go at each other in their respective groups. As all students of AKC lore know, there are six groups, they are judged independently, and sooner or later, depending upon the moods and insights of the judges, a single winner per group is proclaimed. These six, first designated as the best dogs of their respective groups, are the only purebreds to remain in competition. As such, they now face each other at the very highest level found at a point show.

This is the climax of an all-breed point show, and since each of the six finalists is probably the next best thing to a perfect specimen of his or her breed, the competition is sure to be very tough. Often all six are equals, but the judge must find one who is better than the others ("I liked the determined glint in his eyes") and bless that beast as the best darn purebred of all canines at the show. The only survivor is Best In Show (BIS), and the owner's feet won't touch the ground for a week. All owners of the BIS dog's breed, whatever it is and wherever they are, are expected to celebrate.

Earlier, mention was made of the fact that most championship points are won in the classes at the breed level, but that a trio of exceptions does exist. Sometimes either WD or WB can win additional points in the breed, and in rare cases one of them can do more winning at the upper levels.

To appreciate the subtler workings of the AKC championship-point system, let's consider the happy story of Martha Myth, a lovely Airedale bitch who went WB for two points on a rainy day in June. The next thing Martha did was return to the ring to face several Airedale champions and handsome George Cherritree, who had gone WD and picked up three points. To the amazement of all onlookers, the judge selected Martha as BOB. Obviously, this meant that she was superior to George, so she also became BW without argument. Because she was superior, she was also deserving of at least as many points as George; now her total was three instead of two. Exception number one.

As BOB, Martha survived the elimination of all the other Airedales in the show and proceeded to the judging of the terrier group. There she also came out on top as the best of all the terrier beasts on hand. As such, she was certainly deserving of as many points as any other terrier had won back at the breed level. A sufficient number of Cairn bitches had been on hand to make that breed's WB worth four points. As first in her group, Martha increased her total to four. Example number two.

As for example number three: it doesn't happen very often, but nonchamps have been known to go onward and upward to Best In

Show, and that was Martha's day to do so. If she was better than any other purebred at the show, she was certainly entitled to as many points as any other pooch in any breed at the show, and in Golden Retrievers WD had collected five points. So, although she started the day with only two points as WB, she ended up as BIS and went home with five points.

On another day and at a different show and under a breed judge who liked ears set a little higher than Martha's, she might not have won her class, much less the honor of WB. That's the dog game, and that's where determination and luck come in. If he knows he has a worthy dog, a fancier will go to show after show, knowing or hoping that the breed judge will agree. As for the luck part, the conditions must be just right when the agreeable judge is found: there's always the chance that better dogs might be on hand, and one of them will take the points. Then there's a chance that the judge, as honest as anyone and also as fallible, might find his or her winners in dogs whom you wouldn't take home and introduce to your mother. Luck does play a role in the making of champions: a minor role for good dogs, a major role for bums. Happily, there are always more good ones than bums wearing the title.

The training a show dog requires doesn't amount to much. The *heel* and *stand* commands are the only ones most dogs need to know. In the ring, the dog is required to gait on lead at times and to hold the proper stance at other times. The gaiting permits the judge to view the dog's correct or faulty action (movement), and the stance permits a close look at the canine body beautiful.

As regards both sexes of canines, judges look for *typey* dogs—those beasts who closely resemble their written breed standards. In the best of all worlds, every breed judge would correctly interpret a given breed standard, but this isn't that kind of world and foolish arbitration is not unusual. However, every breed judge does look for spirit, which is very difficult to misinterpret, and a sadsack show dog who succeeds is exceptionally lucky.

Any purebred deemed eligible for showing is also approved for the sport of Obedience, and so are most of the other purebreds who can't get close to the breed ring. In this sport, a typey canine's good looks don't hurt, but they don't help, either. It's canine intelligence that counts, and a dog's IQ is proven by the way she performs certain routines. The higher her IQ, the better her chances of earning available degrees.

All AKC breeds, the recognized *and* the miscellaneous, are okay for Obedience and can try for one or more degrees so long as they are not vicious, lame, deaf, or totally blind, and have been on earth at least six months. That means an Obedience dog, unlike a show dog, doesn't have to be normal, nor does he have to comply with the specifications of his breed standard. Thus, a Giant Schnauzer can be overshot, a German Shepherd can be white, a Saluki can stand forty inches, and a Dalmation can be spotless. If the dog is brainy enough, the misfit for the breed ring can be a star in Obedience.

Since so many more dogs are eligible, one might think that there would be far more Obedience dogs than show dogs. That is not the case. There are twenty times as many show dogs, proving, among other less interesting things, that the majority of dog fanciers lack ambition or talent or both. The plain truth is that training a dog for the breed ring is like taking candy from a baby, whereas training for the Big O is anything but simple. Even before the training begins, the dog must have the basic commands down pat and respond alertly. The sit must be square and not sloppy, the come is immediate and true, and the heeling is right on target and without lagging. And those basics are just the beginning, in the sense that everything the dog is asked to do springs from them.

Many fanciers refer to Obedience as a higher education for dogs, and maybe it is. These are the degrees a smart dog can earn:

1. **Companion Dog (CD).** On a pedigree and elsewhere, a show champion with this degree would be listed as *Ch. Hootowl Harry CD.*

2. **Companion Dog Excellent (CDX).** A nonchamp with this degree would be *Misty Sally of York CDX.*
3. **Utility Dog (UD).** *Goofball Guss UD.*
4. **Tracking Dog (TD).** *Sundance Sue TD.*

A dog can't earn a UD before copping a CDX and he can't go for that until he's a full-fledged CD. To put that another way, he must earn the degrees in proper order (as listed), and that makes sense, since the degrees are progressively more difficult to attain.

And then there's the TD. A dog can earn this any old time—before, after or between the others. And she is not under obligation to earn any of the others, so it's owner's choice. When a pet purebred earns all four degrees, the proud owner writes the dog's name as Goofball Gus UDT. This is a brilliant dog, and everybody in the fancy understands that her owner-handler is a super trainer.

TD is a one-shot affair, in that the canine candidate earns it on one try or doesn't. If the dog is a failure, he can always try again on another day. Unlike the other Obedience events, tracking trials must be held away from dog-show grounds and on terrain that is more or less undefiled by people and machines. There's no set procedure for training, and personal inventiveness and imagination are necessities. Adults in almost all the breeds are capable of earning the TD on the first or second try, but the test is usually too tough for those with flat faces. The short-muzzled Pug, Brussels Griffon, Boston Terrier and Bulldog have adequate scenting power and can detect roasted turkey or a bitch in heat at a hundred yards, but they can't usually sniff a newly laid trail. Here's the nitty-gritty of the standard tracking trial for the TD:

Two judges determine the dog's success or failure. The handler cannot guide the dog or signal to him, but a lead of 20 feet or more is permissible, the better to keep the dog from running over the hill and out of sight. The dog is expected to follow the preset, fresh trail (no more than two hours old) of a complete stranger over a distance of not less than 440 yards. At the end of the trail, the dog must find an article (glove, wallet, hat) hidden by the same stranger. The time consumed is unimportant, so long as the dog stays on the job. The pooch cannot loaf, chase a chipmunk, play with his tail, take a nap or bite a judge. In fact, any deviation from the appointed task means that the candidate has flunked. Obviously, this is no place for canine clowns.

A short muzzle does not hamper a dog's tries for the other three degrees. To earn any one of them, the dog performs a series of prescribed exercises under a judge who is very particular about the teamwork of canine and handler. Each exercise is worth a set number of points. The total of those points is 200, and a passing grade is 170. However, the grade of 170 or better doesn't mean a thing if the dog flunked a single exercise by scoring fewer than half the allotted points.

This often happens in the very first CD exercise, Heel on Leash, worth 40 points. All the dog has to do is stay at heel while the handler goes through maneuvers ordered by the judge, and sit at heel whenever the handler halts. But if the dog is listless or sloppy, or if the handler issues too many commands, the dog may end up with 18 points or less than half. That's too bad, and there's no way to get any closer to the CD at this trial, not even if the dog's performance is perfect in the remaining exercises. In that unlikely event, the dog would go home with a score of 178 but no cigars.

The dog who scores 170 or better in the approved manner at any official trial qualifies for a *leg*, and the dog must win three legs to earn the CD degree. An Obedience dog must start with either the TD or CD; the choice is up to the owners, and almost all of them vote for the CD. So if you and your purebred get into Obedience, it's a pretty sure thing that both of you will get your feet wet in CD.

That is reason enough for going into a little detail about the CD exercises. Since they are performed by beginning Obedience dogs, the fancy refers to them as the Novice classes. During the first four classes, the dog (with handler) performs solo in the ring. The final two are done by the group method, and they are the toughest. Herewith, the names of the classes or exercises, the point valuation for each, and (in parentheses) the particular basic commands involved: The nutshell description of the exercises are based on the formal AKC rules and regulations, which are not always as clear as their federal counterparts, but are usually just as wordy:

1. **Heel on Leash,** 40 points (heel, sit). Retreat three paragraphs and reread. The maneuvers include right turns, left turns, about-turns and figure eights, each done at directed speeds such as slow, normal or fast. Leash cannot be used to signal, command or assist dog in any way. Thus, a loose lead that never tightens or jerks is required.

2. **Stand for Examination,** 30 points (stand, stay). The dog stands at attention and holds the pose as the judge examines him. During the exam, the handler stands six feet off and faces the dog. To pick up points, the dog must remain motionless until the judge has departed and the handler has returned and put him at ease. Sounds simple, but it's impossible for a shy dog to succeed.

3. **Heel Free,** 40 points (heel, sit). A repeat of Heel on Leash, but minus the leash and the figure-eight routine.

4. **Recall,** 30 points (sit, stay, come, heel). The dog remains on a sit and stay while his handler marches off about thirty-five feet, then wheels and faces him. On the judge's okay, the handler calls or signals to his dog, who then heads immediately for his handler. The dog ends his approach, without command, by sitting directly in front of the handler, an arm's length away and facing. Then, on command or signal, the dog goes to heel position and sits.

5. **Long Sit,** 30 points (sit, stay). A group exercise that's limited to fifteen dogs and starts in the manner of Recall, with all dogs sitting and facing their handlers from across the ring. Dogs must hold their sits for 60 seconds, whereupon each handler returns to his dog's side. When the judge is darn good and ready, all dogs are put at ease.

6. **Long Down,** 30 points (down, stay). Similar to the above, but dogs stay on a down and the time span is three minutes, during which the average handler prays that his dog will remain motionless as well as down.

The Long Sit and the Long Down are the real tests for new dogs and are the exercises in which most failures occur. A big reason is improper conditioning or lack of training time in an adequate environment. A minute may not seem like a long time for an obedient dog to remain on a sit, especially for a dog who has accomplished the feat during training sessions at home many times, and often for much longer periods. But at a trial, the sittingest dog finds herself in strange surroundings and assailed by a plethora of new and often tempting sights, sounds and smells. What's happening outside the ring is bound to attract the attention, if not the body, of any curious, healthy dog.

Still, the biggest danger to any obedient dog on the Long Sit is every other dog in the ring. More often than not during this 60-second test, one dog will stand and take a stroll, or lie down and roll over, or pay a visit to the beautiful bitch on his left. That's a green light for the others, and one or more of them are pretty sure to follow suit. Those who break their sits are judged to be as guilty as the original sinner who was the cause of their forgetfulness. All are sure bets to fail the examination and not qualify for the leg.

The Long Down is even tougher, for the added reason that it is three times as long. Many dogs reach this point in a trial with 160 or so good points to their credit. They've been steady right along, and they look like sure things to get through these final minutes of easy resting. Then, with only three seconds to go, the Smooth Collie can't resist any longer. He must know if the Lhasa Apso next to him is a dog, a mop or what. The Collie rolls over and sniffs the Apso, and that dog jumps and bumps into the Irish Terrier, who thinks it's about time to play, anyway. Those three—Collie, Apso and Irishman—may be forgiven by their owners, but not by the judge. Zero points to them, and none can earn a leg today.

Up in CDX, those two exercises are repeated in a slightly different way and for longer periods of time: three minutes and five minutes, and the dog's handler leaves the ring and goes out of sight for the durations. All things become more difficult for the dog in CDX, and much more so in UD. A visitor from outer space might conclude that the things on four legs are smarter than the upright things on two.

For freshmen dog fanciers, Obedience is a far more satisfying sport than showing. The very nature of a dog show dictates that there will always be many more losers than winners in the breed ring. Unless they have been trained to jump with joy on command, winning dogs do not react to success and losers are equally nonchalant about defeats. This does not apply to their owners: most take the competition among the dogs very seriously, as if they—not the dogs—were picking up points toward a championship. But fanciers are usually polite, some are charming, and they rarely hit each other over the head in public. Most of the losers let off steam by criticizing the judge's strange concept of breed standards.

The human disposition has always been better at Obedience trials, perhaps because the dog's aren't really competing against each other. Among owners, there's little reason for the "my dog is better than your dog" syndrome. They know all about the many training sessions, the hazards, and the kooky things that can happen at trials. True, the top-scoring canines take home the trophies and the other loot, but they evoke applause, not jealousy. Obedience owners appreciate a job well done.

At least, that's the way it was during the first forty years of Obedience under the AKC wing, and nobody dreamed that the spirit of camaraderie would ever be threatened. Then, as 1977 dawned, the powers that be at the AKC shocked the pioneers of Obedience by yielding to pressures from the sport's zealots and inventing yet another title: Obedience Trial Champion.

Before he can have a go at the title, a dog must earn his UD. Then he goes back to the trials at the Open (CDX) and Utility (UD) levels and shoots for the top two spots among the high scorers. Championship points are awarded for first and second place, the total depending upon the number of dogs in the trial. For Dopey Dan UD to become O.T. Ch. Dopey Dan, the dog must cop 100 points under at least three different judges and win at least three first places (two at one level, one at the other). The point schedule is the same wherever the AKC prevails, and first place (high score) can mean anywhere from 2 to 34 points, with 13 points the most for a second place.

Note that Dopey Dan UD can pick up his championship title without bothering to earn his TD degree. For that reason, the sport's loyalists argue that a UD dog can never be more than an incomplete champion, where only a UDT dog deserves recognition as a real and worthy Obedience champion. There's no debate in Canada, where the CKC has, for many years, bestowed the title of champion on any dog who cops the UD degree. Incomplete or not, it's automatic in Canada. No point system there.

One of the sure results of the new AKC title is that perfect scores of 200 will become more common in Open and Utility as UD dogs are pushed harder in their training. Not too many years ago, top scores were in the neighborhood of 195 and a 200 was a seldom happening. Today, 200 scores occur with more frequency, or at least too often to make headlines. It's not that judges have become more lenient or that the canines have become smarter, but that we now know more about training and more people are willing to take the time and apply the new knowledge.

The easiest and quickest way to pick up that new knowledge is via the group method, often taught by those same private obedience schools or in special classes conducted by kennel clubs, breed clubs, and civic groups. What's learned away from home (once a week) is then rehearsed at home (daily), and within three months, the average purebred, whether six months or ten years old, is ready for a first try at a leg in CD.

If you know what you're doing—and you can learn through reading plus observation at actual trials—it's possible to teach the advanced training at home, and it could take less than three months. The trouble is that most dogs readied in that manner haven't been exposed enough to the real world of the trials: strange people, strange dogs and scores of new and fascinating distractions. The dog who is trained only at home and becomes a perfect performer there can be expected to blow sky high when away from home at a trial. The hour spent away from home at school each week costs very little and is worth far more in terms of correct training, socialization and handling the unexpected with finesse.

These two sports—showing and Obedience—are available in all seasons, mostly on weekends, indoors or out, in every part of the United States where fanciers and purebreds are found. So if you own or intend to own a purebred, you'll find ample opportunity to become a dog fancier via one or both sports. And if that sounds like too much work and you'd prefer to loaf your way into at least a local reputation as a fancier, perhaps Junior Showmanship (JS) is the answer to your prayer.

JS is found at most match shows and a majority of point shows, and the dog game's old-timers aren't quite sure if it's a sport, an activity or an experience. Whatever, it has the official blessing of the AKC, a bushel of rules and regulations, trophies and prizes and a growing army of young supporters. Ten through sixteen are the age ranges for humans, and school grades are unimportant.

What happens in JS? Briefly, it is the breed ring all over again, but in reverse. The object is to find the best dog handlers present. The other big difference is that dogs are of secondary importance and represent many breeds rather than just one. JS amounts to handling skill, and the competition is always pretty much on the same level. There are Novice classes for beginning handlers and Open classes for the more experienced. Those classes are divided into Junior (from ten to under thirteen years old), and Senior (from thirteen to under seventeen years old) divisions.

About the purebreds in JS: any dog eligible for the breed ring is okay here, even if she is not entered in the breed ring at the show. Also, any dog eligible for Obedience is okay, *but only if she is also entered* in Obedience at the show. Of course, ownership is important: the dog must be owned or co-owned by the handler or by anyone in the handler's immediate family: the generous interpretation includes father, mother, brother and sister, and also aunt, uncle, grandfather, great-grandfather, grandmother and great-grandmother, and don't forget stepfather and step-mother, half-brother and half-sister and any other steps and halves in the family tree.

About loafing your way to success in JS: while it's silly to take an untrained dog into JS, a dog owned by somebody else and trained to compete in the breed ring or Obedience already knows all that he needs to know for JS. If that "somebody else" is your mother and she's agreeable, there's nothing immoral or illegal about borrowing the dog for JS. On the other hand, it would be unreasonable to expect instant success without a few practice sessions. The dog won't respond and make you look like an expert unless he is accustomed to your gait, touch, voice, manners and such personal idiosyncracies as stumbling or becoming nervous in public.

Since ambition and enthusiasm are variable qualities, it is impossible to estimate the average cost of becoming and remaining a dog fancier. Still, money is the secret ingredient that keeps dog shows running, and the biggest hunk of it does come from the fanciers who patronize the shows and enter their dogs in the sports. The entry fees are usually the same at any show for breed ring, Obedience and JS, although sometimes the junior entry is cut-rate. These days, $8 to $10 is about average, but big-city shows go higher. Tops in the East for 1977 was the $18 entry fee for the annual two-day show of the Westminster Kennel Club in Manhattan.

A great deal of planning goes into even the smallest point show, and the key to a smooth operation is knowing in advance how many purebreds will be on hand for the gala event. So every show has a closing date, usually about three weeks before the actual day of the show. Entries and fees are mailed to the proper show superintendent, or in a growing number of cases, to the show secretary of the sponsoring club. About a week before the show is held, a confirmed entry and a show schedule arrive in the mail. The schedule is a when-and-where guide to all the action: time and ring for the judging of each breed and ditto for each Obedience event. Dog shows are held rain or shine, and judging waits for neither fancier nor dog. Be there on time or the entry dollars go down the drain.

Entry fees are never waived. Nor are they flexible: if the entry fee for an Irish Wolfhound at the Mud Hollow Kennel Club show is $8, it is sure to be $24 for three Pulik. In consideration of those facts, it's fair to say that the entry fee is the only fixed cost at any show. All other costs are optional: the show's catalog (about $2), food and drink (if you didn't bring any) and whatever you decide to buy from one of the purveyors who sell everything from dog books to booties. There's no need to buy special attire. Most fanciers dress neatly and casually, although about half of the adults would probably be happy to wear any uniform approved by the AKC. None recognizes the cost of getting to and from the shows as part of the expense of being a fancier. After all, if they weren't going to the shows, they would be going other places.

Entry forms for future point shows in a given area are free for the asking at any show you attend. Members of local kennel clubs and any other dog fanciers within reach can either supply the forms or advise you on where to obtain them through the mail. After a purebred has been entered in two or three shows, the owner's name and address pop up on mailing lists and future entry forms are delivered by the postman. The forms are part of an inexpensive handbill known as a premium list. This also includes all the other pertinent data about a given show: the date, place, hours, closing date, judges and the breeds they will judge, Obedience info, trophies per breed, road directions, nearby motels that accept dogs and anything else an inquisitive dog fancier might want to know.

In this country, the traditional goal of the dog fancy has been the improvement of the breeds, meaning the pure breeds of canines. This goal remains, although all of the breeds have long since been improved to everybody's satisfaction. It is now a personal goal. Deep in their hearts, most dog fanciers believe that their dogs are more improved than anybody else's and hope to prove it at the shows.*

Win or lose, show and Obedience dogs are certainly more improved than they were before they started strutting their stuff in public. Now they are more obedient, far less suspicious of strangers, not upset by strange scents and vibrations and friendlier with other canines. And thanks to the expertise of the devoted master or mistress—the fancier—the dog is kept in tiptop shape: well groomed, healthy, properly nourished and cared for, and up to date on shots. The proof of the pudding about good health is that contagious canine diseases do not sweep through dog shows. If a dog's health is suspect, there's always a vet on hand to handle the problem.

Obviously, the purebred who goes to a few shows is more a dog of the world than before and a much more enjoyable pet. And, the dog fancier who manages to accept defeat with the same aplomb

---

*Breed ring and Obedience rules are pretty much the same in Canada, although the championship point system is a little different. See Chapter Nine for where to find booklets on AKC and CKC rules and regulations.

as victory also improves and becomes a better person. Only age can get in the way, but even that can't stop the family from learning a thing or two about patience, courtesy and good sportsmanship.

I have been up to my ears in dogs for a long time and writing about them for some time, and there has been no way to escape knowing dog fanciers in all age groups and by the boatload. Most dog fanciers will admit that their special interest has brought them unexpected pleasures: meeting old friends and making new ones, mingling and exchanging views with people from other walks of life, the enlightening aspects of travel, the development of poise, the joy of knowing that the training was not in vain and a new appreciation of good cooking. (Generally the food available at dog shows is a little worse than pretty bad, and it's usually expensive for such simple fare. It's best and always tastier to bring it from home.)

Families are very much in evidence in the dog fancy, and it's safe to say that very few dog fanciers—the young, the old, the inbetween, and those who lie—are into narcotics, robbing banks, or stealing cars. It's as if true blue fanciers try to be good examples for their dogs.

# 8

# Futures in Dogs

A few years ago I needed to know what dog lovers and fanciers were spending each year on their favorite beasts. Just in the United States, that is. All through a snowbound weekend, I fed tidbits of valid information into my friendly computer, and in due time it arrived at the figure of $7 billion. When published, this figure astounded a great many people in the dog game, but not the manufacturers and sellers of prepared dog foods. In the area of dollars spent, dog food is king of the hill, puppy sales are next, and veterinary fees aren't far behind.

The thing economists don't understand and pet lovers do is that whatever the national economy—good, bad or drifting—the dog business has continued to rise. This has been true since World War II, although the dramatic gains have been made over the last dozen years. One big reason is the canine population explosion, and another is that we are spending more on our dogs for better care and nutrition, to say nothing of such nonsensical items as mink coats, rubber toys, bath oils, outdoor heating pads, elaborate collars, horoscopes, jewelry and people-shaped goodies. And then there are the vanity items, bought by the owners to please themselves: oil paintings, bronze figurines, bumper stickers, Bulldog-shaped pillows, Poodle-head drapes, paw-print bedspreads and dresses and jackets depicting a favorite breed.

Right now the good citizens of this land are spending close to $8 billion a year on dogs, and many major industries won't come close to that level in our lifetime. The dollars spent come close to representing one percent of all consumer spending.

If the money being spent on dogs intrigues you, perhaps it will also inspire you to start thinking about your chances of cutting yourself a piece of the pie. Formal education comes first, of course, but there's no reason why you can't also expand your love for dogs into a genuine knowledge about canines and carry on from there into a career. Earning a living through canine-related work may not be the easiest way to fame and fortune, but tens of thousands of people are earning comfortable livings today in the dog game and they aren't complaining. Most jumped the gap from dog lover to dog fancier while they were in their teens; some did it earlier.

I have never kept records on this, but it seems to me that about 60 percent of the young dog-fanciers I've met over the years thought that they would always be involved with dogs as a hobby. Of the remainder, all of them career-minded, these were their top choices:

**Veterinarian.** There are about thirty thousand active veterinarians in the United States, and if all of them worked twenty-four hours a day, there would still be room for twice as many. The field of veterinary medicine has one of the most acute labor shortages in this land of plenty, and there's absolutely no chance that there will be an adequate supply of them in your lifetime. There are only twenty-two veterinary schools (including three in Canada) on this side of the Atlantic, and they produce about sixteen hundred graduates a year. So, for both men and women, this is a solid-gold career; the starting salary is in the neighborhood of $15,000 and the future is unlimited.

Not all vets engage in private practice. Indeed, some 2,000 are teachers in veterinary schools (see Chapter Nine) and another 12,000 are employed by federal, state and local governments, research laboratories and industry. That leaves 16,000 to take care of our pets and livestock, and the majority are concentrated around cities with populations of 100,000 and more. However, about 2,000 of those vets limit their activities to the needs of livestock. This boils the figure down to 14,000 vets dedicated to the interests of small animals, mostly dogs and cats.

While it is almost impossible for a vet not to make a comfortable living, becoming a veterinarian requires more than good intentions. High school-grades are very important, and the more science courses, the better your chances. Beyond that, all vet schools require two or three college years of preveterinary courses, with the emphasis on mathematics, biology and physics and a Bachelor of Science degree. Four years of college and a B.S. do not guarantee admission to a veterinary school, but they help. Being in the top 10 percent of one's class is a must. Many apply to veterinary schools, but, depending upon the school, few are chosen—almost always less than 25 percent. Dropouts are infrequent.

The traditional veterinarian course takes four years, although some schools are now offering an alternate three-year plan on a trimester system that eliminates summer vacations. The degree is D.V.M. (Doctor of Veterinary Medicine) at all the vet schools except the one at the University of Pennsylvania, where it's V.M.D. A degree holder who intends to go into private practice needs a state license, and to get that he or she must pass a state examination.

**Professional Handler.** In the breed ring, all handlers are divided into two categories: amateur and professional. The amateur handles his or her own dogs, while the professional handles dogs belonging to others and charges a fee for the service, win or lose. Until recently, the biggest difference between the two was that the professionals had to be licensed by the AKC.

As of August 1977, there were seventeen hundred pros (all adults), and about one-half million amateurs (all ages). At any show the pros were sadly outnumbered. Nonetheless, the pros handled about twenty-five percent of the dogs in competition, and usually those dogs did more than fifty percent of the winning.

But in September 1977, the AKC ruled that it would no longer license professional handlers. Supervision had become too expensive and demanding. Since no other governing body in the world has ever licensed professional handlers, the United States is no longer out of step with the international dog fancy. Only the professional handlers are unhappy about the arrangement, but the best of them will still be able to earn upwards of $100,000 a year.

These days, any dog fancier can become a professional, provided that he or she is old enough to understand the AKC show rules, talented enough to be above average as a handler, and persuasive enough to charge another fancier for services rendered. The field is wide open, and it is not necessary to join the Professional Handlers Association or the Professional Handlers Guild.

**Boarding Kennel.** Almost anywhere you go in this country, you'll find dog lovers who complain that there isn't a decent boarding kennel within a hundred miles, or that there is just one, it's usually overbooked, and life would be simpler and happier if there were more. Since they regard their purebreds as very precious cargo, dog fanciers are even more vociferous about the sad state of the boarding kennel situation. I have friends who think that federal funds should be granted for building new kennels and the heck with new highways, bridges and trips to other planets.

Ownership-management of a good boarding kennel comes as close to a no-risk business as we have in the dog game. With the noble assistance of one or both parents, who cover the operation during school hours, numerous young dog lovers are already running kennels and putting the money they make in the bank for college, or expansion or other futures. Some that I've watched have developed small boarding kennels into family businesses in just a few years.

Even if several boarding kennels already exist in your community, there's always room for another one. Provided, of course, that one or two possible hazards can be eliminated: (1) approval of site depends on local zoning (see your Town Clerk); and (2) in some states, a license is required (see the Animal Control Officer of your state). If these hazards are overcome, then all you need is money for construction or conversion, equipment, supplies, local advertising and the like.

The nice part about the boarding business is the profit. Boarding charges vary according to the dog's size (small, medium, large). In my neck of the woods (the fringes of a city of 30,000), a first-rate kennel asks and gets $6 per day for a Great Dane or Saint Bernard. Within an hour's drive are three cities of over 100,000 where the same breeds are charged $10 and $12, and you can be sure that my local boarding kennel gets plenty of business from those cities. Whatever the going rate, it doesn't cost more than 50 cents a day to feed a Great Dane, and all other expenses, aside from labor, are minimal. Is it any wonder that the kennels prefer large dogs?

When a boarding kennel fails, you can be sure that the owner is at fault. Usually she or he doesn't know very much about dog care, nutrition and health, and is too lazy to maintain a clean, attractive environment for the canine customers in the runs. You don't have to be a breed expert to succeed or have much talent as a trainer or a handler, but you must have the welfare of every dog at heart, keep a hawklike watch on every dog's health, and see to it that all get enough room for exercise and stay happy. Run a clean, attractive, sensible kennel and the dog lovers and fanciers in the area will find the road to your door.

The boarding business isn't for everybody, but there is a way to test your wings by getting into the act in a small way. This is the *private boarding kennel plan*, so named because it calls for no more than a private home or apartment and cooperative parents. If you've already raised a pet dog or have taken care of a friend's dog for a few weeks in your home, you are probably qualified for starting a private boarding kennel, and never mind about zoning or a license. Your home becomes a home away from home for other people's housebroken dogs; you are in a position to accept only long-term, friendly boarders, and many owners will be overjoyed to pay special rates. On the other hand, your investment money for kennel and equipment is zero, your only true cost is dog food, and two Pointers at $5 a head mean $70 a week coming in and about $7 going out.

**Professional Groomer.** Oddly, Poodle owners seldom dream of becoming professional groomers, although many spend more money for coat care than they do on their own coiffures. Simple combing and brushing maintain the coats of some breeds; others require only the brush; and still others need clipping, or plucking and shaping. In all the breeds wearing coats requiring some degree of special attention that the dogs themselves are unable to provide, the great majority of owners are just as helpless.

Books abound on the subject of grooming each of the pure breeds; every public library has a few, and it is presumed that anybody who cannot follow the step-by-step, illustrated instructions has difficulty brushing his own teeth. Despite all the literature, friends in the breed who are eager to demonstrate and teach, and mail-order courses, millions of owners prefer to remain ignorant about the art of grooming, and there's absolutely no likelihood that their numbers will ever diminish. Thus, a prosperous future for all sober professional dog groomers is assured.

Professional grooming establishments were not easy to find away from the big cities just twenty-five years ago, but today they are all over the map, and that's why we have so many dogs looking like their breed standards and wearing coats that are at least temporarily free of mats, burrs, dirt, dandruff and fleas. The difficulty remains in finding an excellent groomer. With few exceptions, the top groomers do not run canine beauty parlors. Rather, they are dog fanciers who prefer to take care of their own show dogs, or professional handlers who know just what they want and tailor the grooming for each dog, and aren't about to trust anyone else.

Despite a national grooming association and lobbying in several states, grooming licenses are not required. Thus, some of the pros are better at flimflamming people than clipping dogs. Still, most do a good enough job to keep their customers coming back. The money is fine—rates depend on the local economy—and even the con artists have only a little trouble staying in business. That trouble consists of client turnover, so they are always looking for new dog owners—and finding them.

The booming grooming business owes much of its growth to just one pure breed: the Poodle. Show dogs in each of the Poodle varieties must wear one of three clips just to get into the ring: the fairly simple puppy clip, or the more elaborate saddle and continental clips. While show Poodles don't even amount to one percent of the breed in America, tens of thousands of other Poodles appear in show clips or reasonable facsimiles thereof. It's as if a show clip were a sign of social status for beast and owner. So show Poodles and average Poodles count for a heck of a lot of grooming business.

Still, if it were possible to record all the Poodles wearing show clips, they wouldn't come close to the number of Poodles trotting around in the kennel clip, which is the choice of practical owners and sensible dogs. This is also known as the working, field and home clip. Under any name, it is achieved by scissoring the coat to about one and a half inches (shorter on legs and tail), and it does not necessarily have a topknot or pompom. In this attire, any healthy Poodle looks more like she did in the olden days, or like an honest sporting dog.

All this about the Poodle because it is the one pure breed that you really should know how to clip—if only the kennel clip—if you are thinking of getting into grooming as a sideline now. Of all the ways of earning money in the dog game, grooming is probably the best bet for young dog lovers. At least, more of the dog fancy's teenagers are building bank accounts this way, and the girls outnumber the boys. In the beginning, anyway, you can count on Poodles for most of your business.

The young groomers I know all started in pretty much the same way: learning through books, observation, asking questions and practice. Aside from their own dogs, the practicing was done on dogs owned by friends, relatives, neighbors and willing strangers. They didn't charge for their services—plenty of time for that after they knew what they were doing.

Those are the top career choices of your peers in the dog fancy. Along the way, some will change their minds and wind up in other vocations, but they can always put their special interest to work in their spare time for extra dollars. Except, of course, for those who dream of becoming veterinarians—you can't be a spare-time vet. On the other hand, there's plenty of opportunity (full- or part-time) for *veterinary technicians*, the right hands for overworked vets who need trained help. This requires special training; a growing number of junior colleges are offering courses (usually under the name Animal Technician), and any vet can tell you where the nearest colleges are.

Sometimes dog fanciers discover pleasure and profit by combining hobbies. Thus, the dog fancier who is also a camera bug stands an excellent chance of becoming a superior photographer of canines, because she or he knows what to look for in certain breeds and how to work with the subjects to bring out their best. The same goes for the dog fancier whose artistic bent is portraiture. Our land overfloweth with fair to good photographers, painters and illustrators of dogs, but the excellent ones are few, famous and wealthy.

Some of the youthful fanciers seen at today's dog shows will end up as people who write about dogs in newspapers, magazines and books. More published prose is devoted to the canine than most English teachers imagine, but that doesn't mean that thousands of dog fanciers are pounding typewriters for a living. Most do it for love, not money, and their contributions to canine literature appear mostly in about ten national dog magazines, five times as many specialty (one-breed) magazines, and innumerable breed newsletters. None of the magazines has mass circulation, of course, in the sense of being in a class with *Time* or *Reader's Digest*. Among dog fanciers, the national magazine with status is *Pure-Bred Dogs*, the AKC monthly, while most dog lovers favor *Dog World*.

Some dog fanciers argue that there's no such thing as a professional dog writer anymore, in the sense that a professional writer earns all or the major share of his or her income from the specialty. While that point of view comes close to the naked truth, it is not the whole truth. In all the world, fewer than fifty men and women fit the definition, and their words appear on a regular basis in newspapers or general magazines and sometimes in books. Most were active dog fanciers for many years before turning to writing full-time, an act of faith for most, since it meant leaving established careers in other fields. If only to keep in touch, they remain active in some facet of the dog game, and, quite naturally, more than half are in England. The land that launched the Mayflower has more dogs per capita, more enthusiasm for dogs, and more people in the street who really know dogs than any other country, including the United States.

About half of the fifty have written several dog books, only a very few have more than ten to their credit and most of the works are nonfiction. Overall, the books and their authors seem to prove two things: (1) it is impossible for a single book to cover all that is known about dogs; and (2) the number of writers who manage to get more than a couple of dog books published isn't encouraging for anyone dreaming of a bookish career in the dog game. True, Albert Payson Terhune (1872–1942) wrote more than forty dog books (mostly fiction), but that record has never been broken.

Happily, there's a second echelon of dog writers; in America alone they number in the hundreds, and there always seems to be room for more. Heading the list are those veteran fanciers who write one or two weekly columns for about a hundred daily and Sunday newspapers. Many are career journalists who are already on the newspaper's staff (usually in the sports department), and they write the columns either out of sheer joy or for a bonus. The others are free-lancers who write for flat fees, at per-inch rates, or, when circulation is small, for the pleasure of seeing their bylines. Whatever the fiscal arrangement, the dog columnists are informative, often suspicious of publicity handouts, and well and regularly read. Each is hailed as a canine authority in his or her territory.

Many more fanciers find outlets for their literary endeavors in one of the small publishing firms devoted exclusively to dog books. About 75 percent of the books are devoted to a single breed. The rest deal with such canine subjects as training, health, grooming, handling, horoscopes, herbs, poetry, psychology and naming. The more popular the breed, the more books about that breed, and breeders and judges are eager to write them. As a general rule of thumb, manuscripts are accepted for publication on the basis of the author's background, accomplishments and reputation in the dog game, and writing style is relatively unimportant. Pet stores, booths at dog shows and canine magazines are the normal outlets, and the small flat fees or royalties do not put the authors on easy street. The titles are not usually found in the average bookstore.

So there's plenty of room in any dog fancier's future for writing about dogs and seeing it in print, granted that the fancier has more dependable ways to put bread upon the table. If this sort of writing is your dream, there doesn't seem to be a quick way to achieve success. It does take years to really get to know a single breed, and while you're doing that, you might as well major in English or journalism, and then, after more years in the dog fancy, there will be plenty of time to put what you know about the canine on paper and peddle it.

A casual study of the display and classified ads on the pages of any dog magazine should convince anyone that some dog fanciers stay awake nights plotting new ways to turn their special interest into money-making careers. Let it be noted again, however, that more than half of tomorrow's adult fanciers will be content to grow old with dogs as a hobby while they pursue other, noncanine-related careers. The chances are good that you and most of your peers will support dogs rather than insisting that they support you, and let's hope they'll know and appreciate that and love you even more.

Meanwhile, this is the time to start broadening your knowledge about canines and to gain experience in the dog game. For fun, train for Obedience and the breed ring, and see how far you can go with your pooch. For profit, try something as simple as dog-sitting or dog-walking, or as complex as grooming.

There's a future for you in dogs, but it's up to you—not the dogs. On the other hand, just about any pooch, purebred or Americanis, will be happy to help you find that future and share it with you. Good luck, and as any sentimental German Shorthaired Pointer might say, *Lebewohl!*

# 9

# All the Breeds and Other Matters

It may come as a surprise, but the simple truth is that the Canadian Kennel Club recognizes more pure breeds and varieties than the American Kennel Club. As of 1977, the score was 138 to 122. Many dog fanciers remain blissfully ignorant of that fact, while some of their informed peers argue that the real AKC total is 130. After all, there are those 8 Miscellaneous, which are listed rather than recognized although each is a candidate for future, full recognition.

However, Canadian purebreds are outnumbered by those residing in the United States, and for every two CKC events there are five AKC doggy galas. The AKC has always had more of everything except breeds and—if you insist—equality for women. Since it was founded in 1888, the CKC has always sought women for high office, but the slightly older (by four years) AKC didn't march into modern times until 1974. The CKC has had three women presidents, while the AKC has not yet elected a woman to that office.

The lists that follow are the AKC-recognized pure breeds. If the breed name is in caps, the breed is *not* also recognized by the CKC. If the breed name is in italics, the CKC views the breed in different fashion than does the AKC, and an explanation follows. Breeds recognized only by the CKC are added at the end of each list.

172

# GROUP I: SPORTING DOGS

Pointer
Pointer, German Shorthaired
Pointer, German Wirehaired
Retriever, Chesapeake Bay
Retriever, Curly-Coated
Retriever, Flat-Coated
Retriever, Golden
Retriever, Labrador
Setter, English
Setter, Gordon
Setter, Irish
Spaniel, American Water

Spaniel, Brittany
Spaniel, Clumber
Spaniel, Cocker
Spaniel, English Cocker
Spaniel, English Springer
Spaniel, Field
Spaniel, Irish Water
Spaniel, Sussex
Spaniel, Welsh Springer
Vizsla
Weimaraner
Wirehaired Pointing Griffon

In addition, the CKC recognizes these sporting breeds:

Pointer, German Long-haired
Pudelpointer

Retriever, Nova Scotia Duck
Tolling
Tahltan Bear Dog

# GROUP II: HOUNDS

Hounds were developed to track and trail, or to run down and hold at bay, or to dig in for wild game:

Afghan Hound
Basenji
Basset Hound
Beagle
Black and Tan Coonhound
Bloodhound
Borzoi
Dachshund
Foxhound, American
Foxhound, English

Greyhound
Harrier
Irish Wolfhound
Norwegian Elkhound
Otter Hound
Rhodesian Ridgeback
Saluki
Scottish Deerhound
Whippet

The CKC also recognizes:

Drever                          Finnish Spitz

# GROUP III: WORKING DOGS

These nonunion canine workers evolved as man's loyal helpers and performed (some still do) as herders, guards, guides, haulers of carts and pullers of sleds:

Akita

Alaskan Malamute

Bearded Collie

*Belgian Malinois*

Belgian Sheepdog

*Belgian Tervuren*

BERNESE MOUNTAIN DOG

Bouvier des Flandres

Boxer

Briard

Bullmastiff

*Collie*

Doberman Pinscher

German Shepherd Dog

Giant Schnauzer

Great Dane

Great Pyrenees

Komondorok

Kuvaszok

Mastiff

Newfoundland

Old English Sheepdog

Puli

Rottweiler

Saint Bernard

Samoyed

Shetland Sheepdog

Siberian Husky

Standard Schnauzer

Welsh Corgi, Cardigan

Welsh Corgi, Pembroke

The CKC considers the Belgian Malinois and Belgian Tervuren to be varieties of the Belgian Sheepdog, the only difference being their coats. On the other hand, the CKC prefers to think of the Rough Collie and the Smooth Collie as separate breeds, although their only difference is their coats. Next, a breed that is no longer recognized by the AKC, but is still honored by the CKC:

Eskimo

# GROUP IV: TERRIERS

Most of these activists are natives of England, where they once spent most of their time making life miserable for the rat, fox and badger. Of course, the big ones did double duty as workers:

Airedale Terrier
*American Staffordshire*
   *Terrier*
Australian Terrier
Bedlington Terrier
Border Terrier
Bull Terrier
Cairn Terrier
Dandie Dinmont Terrier
Fox Terrier
Irish Terrier
Kerry Blue Terrier

Lakeland Terrier
Manchester Terrier
Miniature Schnauzer
Norwich Terrier
Scottish Terrier
Sealyham Terrier
Skye Terrier
SOFT-COATED WHEATEN
   TERRIER
Staffordshire Bull Terrier
Welsh Terrier
West Highland White Terrier

In one breed, the CKC clings to the former AKC name, Staffordshire Terrier. Supposedly, adding the word *American* eliminated confusion with Staffordshire Bull Terrier, but fanciers in Canada aren't confused.

# GROUP V: TOYS

Designed as pets and status symbols for the upper classes, the little pooches were also useful as flea catchers in the years before plumbing, soft soaps and daily baths. When the king held his tiny doggy on his lap, his royal (human) fleas jumped to the pet's coat and socialized with canine fleas. The best of those pint-size flea catchers are still with us:

Affenpinscher
Brussels Griffon

Chihuahua
English Toy Spaniel

Italian Greyhound
Japanese Spaniel (or Japanese
   Chin)
Manchester Terrier, Toy
Maltese
Miniature Pinscher
Papillon

Pekingese
Pomeranian
Poodle, Toy
Pug
*Shih Tzu*
Silky Terrier
Yorkshire Terrier

The CKC recognizes the Shih Tzu but places it in the next group. The CKC also gives its blessings to these two:

Cavalier King Charles Spaniel
Mexican Hairless

The AKC lists the Cavalier as miscellaneous, and the hairless wonder is ex-AKC.

## GROUP VI: NONSPORTING DOGS

Most of these breeds can't recall what their ancestors did. Some were never meant to be anything but pets, and a few belong in other groups that are already overcrowded:

Bichon Frise
Boston Terrier
Bulldog
Chow Chow
Dalmation
French Bulldog

Keeshond
Lhasa Apso
Poodle, Miniature
Poodle, Standard
Schipperke
Tibetan Terrier

The CKC puts the Shih Tzu here, and the little pooch is quite sporting about it.

# MISCELLANEOUS

These breeds are listed rather than recognized, and each is a candidate for full AKC membership. To qualify, a breed must prove that it's here to stay, and it does this by attracting a host of loyal breeders and owners who are fairly well distributed across the face of the United States and who are wildly enthusiastic about their favorite breed. The current candidates:

Australian Cattle Dog
Australian Kelpie
Border Collie
Cavalier King Charles Spaniel

Ibizan Hound
Miniature Bull Terrier
Spinoni Italiani
Tibetan Spaniel

The Border Collie and Spinoni Italiani have been standing in line since 1934. The youngest of the candidates is the Tibetan Spaniel who joined the others in 1976.

# VETERINARY SCHOOLS AND COLLEGES

While it's difficult enough getting into any veterinary school or college, it is impossible to get into some unless you are a resident of the same state. This makes Alabama, the only state with two veterinary schools a nice place to live if you want to be a vet. Some veterinary schools do accept out-of-state students, but always on a limited basis, and the quota is not consistent from year to year. Three additional vet schools are now in the planning stages, so a little relief is coming in the future, but that's at least a decade away.

Should you decide to become a veterinarian, start preparing immediately. Hit the books, aim for high grades, and write to the dean of your state's veterinary school or college for the lowdown on the preveterinary courses that are the requirements for admission. If your state lacks a vet school, try writing to the deans of a couple in nearby states. Good luck, and here's the current lineup:

School of Veterinary Medicine
Auburn University
Auburn, AL 36830

College of Veterinary Medicine
Kansas State University
Manhattan, KS 66502

School of Veterinary Medicine
Tuskegee University
Tuskegee, AL 36088

College of Veterinary Medicine
Louisiana State University
Baton Rouge, LA 70803

School of Veterinary Medicine
University of California
Davis, CA 95616

College of Veterinary Medicine
Michigan State University
East Lansing, MI 48823

College of Veterinary Medicine
   and Biomedical Sciences
Colorado State University
Ft. Collins, CO 80521

College of Veterinary Medicine
University of Minnesota
St. Paul, MN 55101

College of Veterinary Medicine
University of Georgia
Athens, GA 30601

College of Veterinary Medicine
University of Missouri
Columbia, MO 65202

College of Veterinary Medicine
University of Illinois
Urbana, IL 61801

New York State Veterinary
   College
Cornell University
Ithaca, NY 14850

School of Veterinary Medicine
Purdue University
West Lafayette, IN 47907

College of Veterinary Medicine
Ohio State University
Columbus, OH 43210

College of Veterinary Medicine
Iowa State University
Ames, IA 50010

College of Veterinary Medicine
Oklahoma State University
Stillwater, OK 74074

School of Veterinary Medicine
University of Pennsylvania
Philadelphia, PA 19104

College of Veterinary Medicine
Texas A & M University
College Station, TX 77843

College of Veterinary Medicine
Washington State University
Pullman, WA 99163

Ontario Veterinary College
University of Guelph
Ontario, Canada

Ecole de Medecine Veterinaire
Universite de Montreal
St. Hyacinthe, Quebec,
    Canada

Western College of Veterinary
    Medicine
University of Saskatchewan
Saskatoon, Saskatchewan,
    Canada

# GOOD READING FOR ALERT FANCIERS

If you intend to become active with your dog in either show or Obedience, boning up on the rules and regulations will make life easier for you. While the sports are conducted in a similar manner under AKC and CKC rules, there are small differences. So, just in case you plan on campaigning your dog on both sides of the border, studying the literature of both governing bodies will reduce the chances of confusion and disappointment. Here's where to write and what to ask for:

American Kennel Club
57 Madison Avenue
New York, N.Y. 10010
(Rules Applying to Registration and Dog Shows; Obedience Regulations)
*Single copies are gratis.*

Canadian Kennel Club
2150 Bloor Street West
Toronto, Canada M6S 4V7
(Dog Show Rules; Obedience Trial Regulations and Standards;
Tracking Test Regulations)
*Single copies are 50 cents each.*

# KEEPING UP WITH AMERICA'S PUREBREDS

Of the many publications devoted to dogs, there are two important ones: *Pure-Bred Dogs, American Kennel Gazette;* and *Dogs in Canada.*

Popularly known as the *Gazette*, the former is the official voice of the AKC. A slick monthly magazine, it's crammed with canine features, news of dogdom, gossipy breed columns, photographs of winning dogs, records of shows and trials and statistics ad infinitum. Most of the prose is listless, but all of it is informative and factual. A one year subscription is $10; sample copy, $2. Same address as AKC.

*Dogs in Canada*, the official voice of the CKC, is a monthly tabloid, and subscribers receive an annual bonus in the form of *Dogs Annual*, which has a slick-magazine format. This publication covers the Canadian scene in much the same manner as the *Gazette*, but it differs in tone—it's editorials are outspoken, the features are lively, and gossip is kept to a minimum. It's a lot for the money. A one-year subscription costs $9 (Canada and USA); sample copy, 75 cents. *Dogs Annual* only (December), $2. Write to 59 Front Street East, Toronto, Ontario, Canada M5E 1B3.

# FINDING THE RIGHT BREEDER

Finding the right breeder is usually as easy as leading a thirsty horse to water. And then there are times—such as June or July—when you know you'll have plenty of summer weeks to take full charge of your new pup but you just can't locate a single litter in the breed of your choice, or at least a litter old enough for new homes.

For a backup list of breeders to contact just in case you exhaust known sources, the names and address of almost all the national breed clubs and the paid advertising of breeders in good standing can be found in both the *Gazette* and *Dogs in Canada*. Send for a samply copy of either, and don't forget to enclose payment.

Or try the economy way: write to "Breeder's Aid" at the *Gazette* or "Breeder Information" at *Dogs in Canada* and request the name of the breeders nearest your home. Don't forget to name the breed of your choice, and a self-addressed, stamped envelope will be appreciated.

In a few breeds, planning ahead is a good idea, since pups are often reserved in advance and litters can be sold out before they've been whelped. There are some breeds that are not always easy to find. But don't despair; information about those breeds can be found at the addresses that follow. Address letters to the secretaries of the following:

Bearded Collie Club of America
P.O. Box 7
Limerick, PA 19468

Bernese Mountain Dog Club of America
Route 1, Box 342
Oostburg, WI 53070

Finnish Spitz Club of America
290 Bennett Road
Hamden, MA 01036

Greater Swiss Mountain Dog Club of America
Carinthia, R. 3
Lafayette, IN 47905

Nova Scotia Duck Tolling Retriever Club of Canada
Box 6172
Fort St. John, British Columbia UJ 487
Canada

Portuguese Water Dog Club
233 West Islip Road
West Islip, NY 11795

Puli Club of America
Pebbletree Farm
Route 3, Brown Road
Whitewash, WI 53070

Soft-Coated Wheaten Terrier Club of America
1168 83rd Street
Brooklyn, NY 11228

Tibetan Terrier Club of America
Rt. 1
Great Falls, VA 22066

Americanis Society of North America
Floating address. Check your vet for healthy pups with gentle
dam and sire. If none are available, ask the vet to recommend the
best of the nearby animal shelters or humane societies. Poorest
sources (in ascending order): strangers, friends and relatives, pet
stores and dog pounds.

# CANINE ANATOMY AND MEASUREMENT

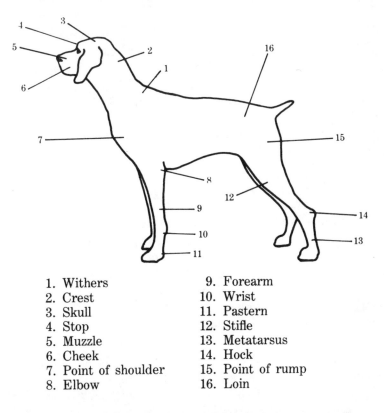

1. Withers
2. Crest
3. Skull
4. Stop
5. Muzzle
6. Cheek
7. Point of shoulder
8. Elbow
9. Forearm
10. Wrist
11. Pastern
12. Stifle
13. Metatarsus
14. Hock
15. Point of rump
16. Loin

Height is measured from the withers (top of shoulders), not from the top of the dog's head. Unless otherwise specified in a breed standard, length is measured from point of shoulder to point of rump.

Technically, *short-coupled* means a short length of back (withers to tail set). However, in the dog game, it means a canine body that is equally tall and long; in profile, the body proper is boxlike, squarish.

For a quick estimate of a dog's proportions, blot the head and tail from your view.

# GLOSSARY of EVERYDAY TERMS

ACTION — Dog's movements, locomotion, gait

ADULT — Older than twelve months

AKC — American Kennel Club, purebred headquarters for the United States

BANDY — Bowlegged up front (Bulldog)

BITCH — Female canine, any age

BITE — Determined by position of upper and lower incisors when jaw is closed.

**even** or **level**—edge to edge

**overshot**—uppers overlap

**scissors**—lowers touch insides of uppers

**undershot**—lowers project beyond uppers

BLOOM — Gloss of coat in prime condition

BLOWN — Coat in bum condition

BOBTAIL — Naturally tailless or docked short (Old English Sheepdog)

BONE — Substance, girth of leg

BOSSY — Overdeveloped up front: chest, neck, shoulders

BREECHES — Trailing portion of thighs under tail

BREED — Dogs of uniform type

BUM — Dog out of uniform, hardly resembles his breed

BUTTOCKS — Rump

CAPE — Coat hairs behind shoulders (Schipperke)

CASTRATION — Surgery to remove testicles, neutering the male

CHARACTER — Approved personality, temperament

CKC — Canadian Kennel Club, overseer of purebreds in Canada

COAT COLORS — Novice dog lovers are sometimes confused by these terms.

**belton**—white hairs intermingled with basic color to produce blue belton orange belton and so one.

**biscuit**—bread crust or light rust

**blue**—really a blue-gray

**blue merle**—blue mixed with black

**brindle**—a 50–50 mix of light and dark hairs

**dappled**—mottled markings on basic color

**deadgrass**—sedge or old straw

**flecked**—or ticked, a sprinkling of darker hairs

**foul color**—inappropriate for the breed

**grizzle**—Bluish with a heavy sprinkling of gray

**hound-marked**—white, black and tan combo found on hounds (Beagle)

**Isabella**—fawn

**lemon**—light yellow

**orange**—light tan

**parti-color**—two colors

**self-color**—solid and sometimes with shadings

| | |
|---|---|
| COBBY | Close-coupled, boxlike |
| CONFORMATION | Proper body structure for the breed |
| CORKY | Spirited, zippy |
| CREST | Arched upper part of neck (Collie) |
| CROPPING | Surgery to reshape a dog's ears for show (Bouvier) |
| CROSSBREED | Each parent is from a different pure breed; an Americanis |
| CRY | Noise of hound following a trail |
| DAM | A pup's mother |
| DEWCLAW | An extra, useless toe found in some breeds (Puli, Great Pyrenees) |
| DISTEMPER | Common virus disease, easy to prevent |
| DOCKING | Surgery to shorten tail (Irish Terrier) |
| DOG | Either sex, but always means *male* in competitions |

DUDLEY NOSE    Flesh-colored
EARS           Worn by every breed, either natural or
               cropped
  **bat**—wide base, erect, orifice to the front (French Bulldog)
  **button**—folded forward covering orifice (Fox Terrier)
  **flying**—sprawling, a no-no on any breed
  **drop**—long and hanging (Bloodhound)
  **hanging**—a modified drop ear (Flat-Coated Retriever)
  **prick**—erect, tip rounded or pointed (Samoyed)
  **semi-prick**—erect and tip leaning forward (Collie)
  **rose**—small, hanging and folding backward (Bulldog)
EASY KEEPER    A pooch who always enjoys meals
ECZEMA         Wet or dry; a common inflammation of
               the skin
EXPRESSION     The head (eyes, ears, face) is typical of
               breed
FALL           Fringe of hair overlaps face (Bearded
               Collie)
FANCIER        A dog lover flying high
FEATHER        Fringe of hairs on back of legs, under
               tail (English Setter)
FINISHED       Dog has won his show championship or
               Obedience degree; still eligible to
               compete
FOREFACE       Muzzle
GAIT           The way a dog moves along
HEAT           A bitch's season or time for mating
HEPATITIS      A serious liver disease; preventative
               shots are musts
INCISORS       Front teeth: six uppers, six lowers
JUDGE          Breed and Obedience judges approved
               by the AKC and CKC
KENNEL         Home for one dog or one thousand dogs
KENNEL-BLIND   Anyone who refuses to recognize his or
               her dog's faults

| | |
|---|---|
| KISSES | Tan spots over eyes, on cheeks (Gordon Setter) |
| LEAD | Leash |
| LEATHER | Ear flap |
| LEGGY | Legs too long for breed |
| LEPTOSPIROSIS | Acute kidney disease; preventable by injection |
| LITTER | Family of pups |
| LUMBER | The degree of overweight |
| MONGREL | Either both parents are of mixed ancestry or just one is; a true Americanis |
| MUZZLE | The face from eyes to nose |
| OCCIPUT | Top point of skull |
| OFA | Orthopedic Foundation for Animals |
| PACING | The legs on same side move in unison (Old English Sheepdog) |
| PEDIGREE | The family tree or ancestral record of any dog, purebred or Americanis |
| PUPPY | Under twelve months |
| PUREBRED | The dog's Mom and Pop are members of the same pure breed |
| PUT DOWN | Groomed and ready for show, parade or church picnic |
| RACY | Tall, slim and streamlined |
| RINGERS | Pooches who look like identical twins |
| RUFF | Profuse coat around neck (Chow Chow) |
| SADDLE | Black markings on back |
| SIDEWINDER | A dog who gaits at an angle, crablike |
| SIRE | A pup's father |
| SNIPEY | The muzzle is narrow, too sharp overall |
| SOUND | Intelligent and healthy |
| SPAYING | Preventive surgery to prevent motherhood |
| STANCE | The approved standing position |
| STANDARD | Written blueprint for the ideal dog of a given pure breed; better known to purists as breed standard |

| | |
|---|---|
| STERN | Tail |
| STILTED | Choppy gait |
| STOP | Step up from muzzle to skull; the indentation found between the eyes of many breeds |
| TEAM | Quartet of dogs of the same breed |
| TIMBER | Degree of leg bone |
| TUCK-UP | Small waist (Dalmation) |
| TYPEY | A dog who looks like his or her breed standard |
| UNTHRIFTY | In poor health on a continual basis |
| WEEDY | Insufficient timber |
| WHELPING | The birthing time of pups |
| WHELPS | Unweaned pups; up to four weeks, in most breeds |
| YAPPER | A foolish, frequent barker |
| YEANLING | A Bedlington Terrier pup |
| ZOTT | A purebred who is so unlike his or her breed standard that the dog really isn't worth a zott, whatever that is |

# Index

189

## THE AUTHOR

KURT UNKELBACH admits to having been a sincere failure in several careers before becoming a Madison Avenue executive and then finally fleeing to the hills to write about more important matters than fashion, cosmetics and travel. Since then, he has become America's most widely published author of canine-oriented books.

His fiction includes such novels as *Love on a Leash*, *The Dog in My Life*, and *Uncle Charlie's Poodle*. His most recent nonfiction works are *The American Dog Book* and *How to Show Your Dog and Win*. Mr. Unkelbach is also the original biographer of Albert Payson Terhune, is responsible for several cat books, and holds the Fido Award, dogdom's equivalent for the Academy Award for writing.

The author and his wife (also a writer) are veteran breeders, trainers and exhibitors of Labrador Retrievers, and their line-bred Walden strain is behind many of today's outstanding breeding programs.